HOW TO COME TO THE UK

To Live Work Study or Visit

HOW 2 COME TO THE UK

To Live Work Study or Visit

Charles Kelly & Cynthia Barker
Registered Immigration Advisers

CAMPION BOOKS

Copyright © Charles Kelly & Cynthia Barker 2005

Charles Kelly & Cynthia Barker have asserted
their right under the Copyright,
Designs and Patents Act, 1988, to be identified
as the authors of this work.

All rights reserved.
No part of this publication may be reproduced, stored in a
retrieval system, or transmitted in any form or by any means,
electronic, mechanical, photocopying, recording or otherwise,
without prior written permission of the author.

A catalogue record for this book
is available from the British Library

ISBN 0-9546338-3-0

All illustrations by Jan Alvey

Printed in the UK

First published in the UK in 2005 by

CAMPION BOOKS
2 Lea Valley House
Stoney Bridge Drive
Waltham Abbey
Essex, UK
EN9 3LY

www.how2cometotheuk.com

This book is dedicated to
all the hardworking immigrants
who arrive in the UK with
'nothing to declare'
except their brains, talents, energy,
and burning desire to succeed.

Publisher's Notice

Immigration Law is a complex subject, covering a vast number of rules over a wide area encompassing: Work Permits, Family Settlement, and Entry Clearance. This book is intended as an overview of the many opportunities to come to the UK and as a general guide to procedures.

Immigration Rules are constantly changing. We recommend that you always check the Home Office UKvisas website for full details and/or consult your legal adviser.

The aim of this book is to give an overview and to show that there are many options for those seeking to come to the UK to live, work, study or visit if they are prepared to gather information, make a plan and take the right action at the right time.

We have set out to write an easy-to-follow general guide to the types of schemes available rather than a textbook on immigration law. We have not covered asylum because this is a vast subject requiring a book in its own right.

Whilst every care has been taken in the preparation of this book, neither the publishers nor the authors are liable for any consequences of any action or advice taken.

You are advised to always seek professional advice from a registered, qualified immigration adviser who will be able to advise you on the specifics of your own case.

Contents

	Introduction	**11**
	The UK Needs People – Points to Ponder	**12**
Chapter 1	**H O W 2 Come To The UK to Work - Main Schemes**	**19**
	Work Permits – Overview	19
	Ordinary Work Permits	25
	Tier 1 - Shortage Occupations	25
	Tier 2 - Non-Shortage Occupations (Tier 2)	26
	Training & Work Experience Scheme (TWES)	27
	Other	28
	Multiple Entry Work Permits	28
	Letters of Approval	28
	Other Schemes & Arrangements	29
	Sector Based Scheme (SBS)	29
	Highly Skilled Migrant Programme (HSMP)	31
	Seasonal Agricultural Workers Scheme (SAWS)	34
	Intra-Company Transfers (I-CT)	35
	Working Holidaymakers Scheme	36
	Worker Registration Scheme	39
	Special Feature: Work Permits for Nurses	39
	Four Simple Steps – From Job Offer to Travel	42
Chapter 2	**H O W 2 Come To The UK for Business**	**43**
	Business Persons	43
	Sole Representatives	45
	Investors	46
	Innovators	51
	EC Association Agreement	53

Chapter 3	**H O W 2 Come To The UK to Study** **54**	
	Overseas Students 54	
	Student Nurses 57	
	Overseas Doctors/Dentists taking (PLAB) tests 58	
	Postgraduate Dentists and Doctors 59	
	Re-sitting Students 60	
	Students Writing Up a Thesis 61	
	Students' Union Sabbatical Officers 63	
	EEA Students 63	
	Working Whilst Studying 65	
	Switching to Worker Status 68	
	Working after your Studies in the UK 69	
Chapter 4	**H O W 2 Come To The UK to Settle** **75**	
	Partner, Husband, Wife, Fiancé or Fiancée 75	
	Children 78	
	Adopted Children 79	
	Parents, Grandparents & Other Dependant Relatives 81	
	Investors 84	
	Indefinite Leave to Remain / Permanent Residency 84	
	British Citizenship / Naturalisation 86	
Chapter 5	**H O W 2 Come To The UK as a Visitor** **89**	
	Visitors 89	
	Tourist Visitors 90	
	Academic Visitors 92	
	Business Visitors 93	
	Medical Treatment Visitors 95	
	Student Visitors 97	
	Cruise Passenger / Transit Visitors 97	
	Carer Visitors 98	
	Marriage & Fiancé(e) Visitors 98	
	Relatives Acting as Childminders Visitors 100	
	Persons Coming for Job Interviews 101	
	Minister of Religion Visitors 101	
	Visitors taking part in Archaeological Digs 102	
	Amateur Entertainers & Sportspeople 102	
	Applicants Seeking Re-Admission to Attend Appeal Hearings 102	

Chapter 6	**H O W 2 Come to the UK – Other Schemes**	**103**
	Permit-Free Employment	103
	Domestic Workers	104
	Visitors Exercising Access Rights to UK Resident Child	105
	Entertainers	106
	Postgraduate Doctors & Dentists	108
	Science & Engineering Graduate Students	110
	Ministers of Religion	112
	Film Crew on Location	113
	Representatives of Overseas Media Organisation	114
	Overseas Government Employees	115
	JAPAN Youth Exchange Scheme	115
	Sportspeople	116
	Gap Year Entrants for Work in Schools	118
	Voluntary Workers from Overseas	119
	Fresh Talent Working in Scotland Scheme	120
	Citizens of EEA, Switzerland and the UK	122
	Workers Registration Scheme – New EU Member States	123
	Au Pairs	124
	Writers, Composers & Artists	126
	Airport-Based Operational Ground Staff of Overseas Airlines	126
	Teachers and language assistants coming to the UK under approved exchange schemes	127
	Special Cases – e.g. Turkey, Bulgaria…	127
Chapter 7	**H O W 2 Apply for Visas & Entry Clearance**	**128**
	Visas - General	128
	Entry Clearance – Facts & Figures	130
	Information Applicable to all Visas and Entry Clearance	131
	Visitors	134
	Work Permit Holders	135
	Domestic Worker Visits	136
	Business or Employment-Related Visits	136
	Working Holidaymakers	138
	Visitors Getting Married but not Settling	139
	Academic Visitors	140
	Medical Treatment Visitors	142
	Foreign Armed Forces Personnel Visitors	143
	Visitors in Transit	143
	Settling in the UK	145

Chapter 8	**H O W 2 Get Started**	**146**
	Action Plan	146
	Getting Started on Your Action Plan	148
	Working or Studying in the UK – Getting Started	151
	NARIC	151
	IELTS	152
	Students – The First Steps	153
	Workers – The First Steps	156
	Five Sources to Help You Find a Job	158
	Seven Tips on Writing & Presenting Your CV	159
	Visiting the UK – The First Steps	161
	Settling in the UK – The First Steps	162
	Useful Contacts	163
	Really Useful Websites	169
Appendix 1	SBS – List of jobs for which work permits can be issued	171
Appendix 2	List of Shortage Occupations for work permits	172
Appendix 3	Who does not require a work permit?	174
Appendix 4	Worker Registration Scheme	176
Appendix 5	More Information for Au Pairs	176
Appendix 6	Science and Engineering Graduate Scheme – Eligible Subjects at each Level of Study	177
Appendix 7	More about the innovators application process	180
Appendix 8	More about medical visitors	181
Appendix 9	Visa Nationals	183
Appendix 10	Information on the Right of Abode	187
Appendix 11	Sample HSMP Calculator	192

INTRODUCTION

Why We Have Written This Book

Over many years as Immigration Advisers we have encountered thousands of people who have not had the right advice when they needed it, and have therefore spent unnecessary time and money going down the wrong roads to successfully entering the UK.

Most people are not aware that there are so many ways of legally entering the UK to live, work, visit, or study, and we wanted to bring this to the attention of the millions of people who would otherwise have neither easy access to, nor a good understanding of, this information.

We would like to share our knowledge in a unique 'HOW 2' guide format.

We hope you find it useful.

Charles Kelly & Cynthia Barker

UK Needs People – Points to Ponder

Past, Present and Future

PAST

From times since before the Romans, Britain has been built on the efforts of immigrants, whether they came as conquerors, refugees, or simple seekers of a better life in these Islands of Opportunity which have become known as the United Kingdom.

In the 20th century, Commonwealth citizens came to the UK bringing a wide cultural diversity and many skills with them, as well as a great deal of energy and commitment to succeed.

Restrictions of foreigners seeking work in the UK were first introduced during the First World War. In 1919-20 a system of work permits was brought in which laid down conditions to regulate the employment of non-commonwealth foreigners.

The need to rebuild a shattered economy after 1945 led to labour shortages. Between 1945 and 1950, about 170,000 displaced citizens from Eastern Europe were placed into employment, as well as another 136,000 foreigners with work permits, the latter being mostly from Western Europe.

Between the end of the Second World War and the late 1960s, there was a fluctuating upward trend in work permits issued. Most work permits went to unskilled and semi-skilled workers: during the 1950s, the largest category was domestic service, 44 per cent of the total in 1955. A growing number of permits were granted for nurses, doubling to 2,400 between 1950 and 1955.

The Commonwealth Immigrants ACT of 1962 brought labour

immigration from the Commonwealth under some kind of control. From 1 January 1972, work permits were not issued for unskilled and semi-skilled foreign labour from outside the EEC. The 1971 Immigration Act further tightened controls by putting the issue of work permits for Commonwealth citizens on the same basis as for non-EEC foreign nationals. For a permit to be issued, an overseas worker now had to have both a specific job to come to, and a skill or qualification that was needed. A prolonged period of decline in work permits issued followed to around 15,000 during the early 1980s. In 1982, the number of long-term work permits granted was only 5,700.

From the mid-1980s, the number of work permits began to rise significantly, peaking in 1990 at around 30,000. More recently, a wider range of immigrants have sought to bring their much-needed skills to the UK – including many thousands of highly skilled nursing and healthcare staff – so that 2002 saw the issue of nearly 130,000 approved work permits.

In May 2004, ten new member states (Poland, Lithuania, Latvia, Estonia, Cyprus, Malta, Poland, Slovenia, Slovakia, and the Czech Republic) were admitted to the European Union. The UK was one of the few countries to allow free labour movement and, in a recent report by The BBC, it is estimated that around 130,000 people from the new member states have come to seek work in the UK in the last 12 months.

PRESENT

The Home Office, which is headed by The Home Secretary, Mr Charles Clarke, is a government department which regulates immigration into the UK. The specific department within the Home Office is the Immigration and Nationality Directorate (IND), which has control of: Work Permits; Asylum; Appeals; Nationality; Permission to Stay; as well as Border Controls and Law Enforcement.

The UK government is seeking to encourage managed

migration to fill the skills gaps that exist in the UK job market. It is recognised that the UK needs doctors, dentists, nurses, teachers, and many more workers. The government understands that, without legal, managed migration, many of our public and private organisations and institutions would continue to have serious skills gaps and therefore struggle to maintain services.

Some of the most pressing skills gaps have been in the nursing, healthcare and teaching fields. However, there are thousands of work permits issued each year for such diverse occupations as chefs, domestics, waiters, and other catering staff, as well as highly skilled specialist occupations like IT programmers, dentists, and doctors.

The UK Home Office has established two new sector-based schemes for the hospitality and manufacturing sectors, designed to allow 20,000 permits to be issued. (See **Sectors Based Scheme (SBS)** in *Chapter 1*.)

The Home Office has also introduced a separate programme, designed to attract the top talent to the UK, called the Highly Skilled Migrant Programme (HSMP). This is good news for skilled professional people from overseas wishing to enter the UK to find work without having to find an employer to sponsor them. See **Highly Skilled Migrant Programme (HSMP)** in *Chapter 2*.

FUTURE

Whilst potential migrants may have been alarmed and dismayed by calls from UK political parties to 'get tough' on immigration, the facts are that all parties accept that the UK needs overseas workers to fill skills gaps and maintain a vibrant and thriving economy. Both applicants and employers can take comfort from the outlook for the future of immigration in the UK, as presented in a speech by Charles Clarke, the Home Secretary, in 2005...

> *'The Government's approach is to have tough measures to tackle abuse of the asylum system and illegal immigration, while at the same time working to build tolerance and enthusiasm for legal, managed migration.'*
>
> *'No modern, successful country can afford to adopt an anti-immigration policy.'*
>
> *'It is in all our interests to harness the innovation, skills, and productivity that new migrants can bring.'*
>
> *'Migrants make a disproportionate contribution to the wealth of the UK, accounting for eight per cent of the population but 10 per cent of the gross domestic product. Home Office research has shown that legal migrants contribute £2.5 billion more in taxes than they consume in services and they have little or no adverse affect on the wages or employment levels of the existing population.'*
>
> *'Migration is only one facet of the broader phenomenon of globalisation which is shaping the modern world. If we are to achieve flexibility and sustainable growth, then legal migration... must be the way forward.'*

The government has announced plans to overhaul the work permits system. The emphasis will be on attracting more highly skilled people to the UK and reducing lower skilled migration from outside the European Union.

Home Secretary Charles Clarke said: 'The route to settlement is through skilled labour. This means that the more skilled you are, the more likely you are to be able to stay.'

The shift from a UK work permit system for migrants to one based on points over five years is the major change in approach. Under the new Australian-style scheme, the more skills a person has, the more points they will gain, increasing their likelihood of entry to the UK.

The United Kingdom is the fourth largest economy in the world, and has a population of 58,789,194 million people (on Census Day 2001 – source: www.statistics.gov.uk). London is the largest city in the EU with a population of over 7 million, attracting over 11 million tourists every year.

The age structure of the UK population has become older in the last three decades, and will become older still in the next three decades, due to a decline in the numbers of children born. This has led to a declining proportion of the population aged under 16, and an increasing proportion aged 65 and over. The percentage of older people (aged 65 and over) increased from 13 per cent in 1971 to 16 per cent in 2003 and is projected to rise to 23 per cent in 2031.

In other words, birth rates are going down and people are living longer in retirement. Based on current trends, the working population will not be able to generate sufficient wealth to support the retired population. More 'wealth generators' are needed. (source: www.statistics.gov.uk)

A Land of Opportunity

The UK is full of opportunities to find employment, study, or start a business. The benefits of living in the UK include free education for children, free healthcare through the NHS, and other state benefits such as Pensions. More importantly, you will enjoy the benefit of living in a democratic and free society. There are literally thousands of 'rags to riches' success stories of people who came to the UK with 'nothing to declare' apart from their brains, talent, and a burning desire to succeed.

Michael Howard, the Conservative Party leader, came from a family of first generation immigrants to the United Kingdom and he almost became Prime Minister in the recent general election. In other words, anything is possible! However, do not expect that the doors to the UK will simply be thrown wide open. The road to living, working, or studying in the UK will continue to be full of hurdles. Those best equipped for the road ahead will be the ones who reach the final destination.

Knowledge is power. Read this book!

"Logic will get you from A to B.
Imagination will take you everywhere."
Albert Einstein

www.immigrationmatters.co.uk

SUCCESS STORY

Raj came to London from India in the 1970s on a student visa to study Law. After qualifying as a Barrister and building a successful career in law, he began to feel that the 'mundane' legal field was not for him. Having just bought a property at an auction he caught the 'bug' and immediately quit his job to go into the far riskier, but more exciting world of property development. At the time, his father and fellow Lawyers thought he was insane! Undeterred, Raj worked hard for the next few years. Buying and selling, reinvesting his profits, and using the bank's money to finance further deals.

Raj proved he was anything but insane and has built up a multi-million pound fortune with a portfolio of over 100 properties in London.

SUCCESS STORIES

Jaybee, pictured here with her family, came to England as a single person and obtained a Work Permit. Jaybee later got married and, with the help of Charles Kelly and Cynthia Barker, processed her husband's Dependant Visa. Jaybee and her husband have since had a beautiful baby girl, and Charles and Cynthia have again been successful in obtaining a visa.

Five years ago Greg came to UK to attend a job interview at T-mobile as Senior Cell Planning Engineer. He passed the interview and brought back with him the necessary documents to be presented at the British Embassy in Manila, Philippines. He was then granted entry clearance together with his family who joined him in the UK. After four year of continuous work Greg successfully applied for his permanent residency (Indefinite Leave to Remain) and will shortly apply for British Citizenship and will avail of dual citizenship.

Chapter 1

H O W 2 Come to the UK to Work
– Main Schemes

WORK PERMITS

By far the most popular route

AT A GLANCE:

- ◆ Granted by the Home Office
- ◆ Gives holder permission to work in a specified occupation in UK
- ◆ Gives holder permission to work in for a defined period
- ◆ Employer applies for a work permit on behalf of the employee
- ◆ Application should be for a named person to do a specific job
- ◆ A genuine vacancy must exist
- ◆ You can apply to bring your dependants

GENERAL

Nationals of European Economic Area (EEA) countries as well as certain other citizens and some dependants of work permit holders do not require a work permit. (See *Appendices*.)

However, other people want to come to the UK to work, and the UK wants them to come. The work permit scheme allows UK employers to recruit or transfer people from outside the European Economic Area (EEA) while still protecting the interests of resident workers in the UK. (The scheme also allows overseas nationals to come to the UK for training or work experience).

Most non-EEA nationals need a work permit
Any non-EEA national seeking entry or permission to remain in the UK for the purpose of employment will normally require a work permit. In other words, any person outside the European Economic Area – for example, America, China, India, and The Philippines – will need to obtain a work permit in order to work in the UK.

Some non-EEA nationals can come without a work permit
The Immigration Rules allow people to come to the UK for certain types of employment *without* a work permit. For example, see sections on: permit-free employment; setting up in business; investors; working holidaymakers; au pairs; overseas domestic workers.

There are various types and categories of work permit
The various types of work permits can be divided into categories such as *Ordinary*, *Multiple Entry*, *Letters of Approval,* and *Other Schemes & Arrangements* (see below).

Work permits are issued by Work Permits (UK), part of the Home Office's Immigration and Nationality Directorate (IND).

A work permit relates to a specific person and a specific job. It gives the holder permission to work in a specified occupation in the UK for a defined period and is by far the most popular route for migrants entering the UK.

Employers apply for a work permit on behalf of a named employee to do a specific job for the employer, normally on a full-time basis.

The Home Office does not issue Work Permits for Self-Employment or Unskilled Jobs. However, there are ways in which you can still enter the UK to start a business, employ yourself, or take up unskilled work.

PLAN OF ACTION

You should check that your status allows you to work in the UK before taking up employment. Not everyone who comes to the UK is allowed to work, and employers face heavy fines for employing anyone not authorised to legally work. You can check if you are allowed to work by looking at the stamp in your passport.

Your status may only allow you to stay in the UK for a limited time. In some cases, when the time is finished, you cannot apply to stay longer. If you are eligible to extend your stay in the UK, you will need to make an application before your original permission ends. For example, if you are here in the UK on a 2-year work permit and would like stay on for a longer period, you must either extend or renew that permit at least 6 weeks before the expiration date of the work permit and visa (this period can vary according to Work Permits UK published service levels). If you miss the deadline, you will have to return home and apply for entry clearance to come back to the UK.

The same applies if you are changing employers. Your new employer must apply for the work permit in good time. When changing employers you need to ensure that your prospective employer will be able to obtain a work permit on your behalf. Whilst this may sound obvious, as immigration advisers, we often come across cases where a worker has left their original employer (who has a duty to cancel the work permit), only to discover later that the new employer cannot obtain a work permit on their behalf. They then find themselves in 'no man's land' where their work permit has been cancelled and they have no new permit to replace it. As you will see below, obtaining a work permit requires both employee and employer to meet the requirements, and just because you have a work permit with employer A, it does not necessarily follow that you will automatically obtain one from employer B.

Work Permit Criteria
The full requirements can be found on the Home Office website. In general terms, the Home Office will normally only approve work permit applications for jobs which require people with either a UK equivalent degree level qualification (see NARIC); or a relevant HND level qualification; or a HND level qualification that is not relevant, plus one years' relevant work experience; or at least 3 years full time relevant experience at NVQ level 3 or above.

There are exceptions such as the Sector Based Scheme which is aimed at lower skilled workers and is covered in more detail later in this chapter. However, the main thrust of any country's 'Managed Migration' scheme is to attract the right people to fill the skills gaps that exist in the job market. You will note that people coming in under the Sector Based Scheme are limited to one year's stay at a time and will not generally qualify for permanent residency.

Under the 'Managed Migration' plan, certain occupations are encouraged more than others and there are points systems for certain applicants.

Employer Requirements
The employer will also have to satisfy Home Office requirements

when applying for a work permit. For instance, employers are often asked to provide their latest set of accounts and evidence of trading. Employers may also have to show evidence that a 'genuine vacancy' exists and that they cannot fill this vacancy from the resident labour pool. The job will also need to meet the work permits criteria. The requirements can vary according to the type of application and whether or not the employer has applied for a work permit in the past.

Employee Requirements

The exact requirements will depend on the scheme for which you are applying. In most cases, the main things you will need to provide relate to academic or educational attainment (diplomas or degree certificates) and work experience (detailed work references from past employers).

Certificates gained on seminars or short courses may assist your application, but are not usually recognised by the Home Office as a qualification, and will not, therefore, qualify you to obtain a work permit. One example is the short courses taken by previously unqualified people in caring for the elderly in the hope that this will help them obtain a work permit. Unfortunately, the majority of these candidates have little or no additional experience in the caring profession and will not be able to obtain a work permit in the UK.

The work permit criteria states that work permits will normally be granted for people with UK equivalent degree level qualification; or a relevant HND level qualification; or a HND level qualification that is not relevant, plus one years' relevant work experience; or at least 3 years full time relevant experience at NVQ level 3 or above. A NARIC assessment will compare your qualification with a UK equivalent, and determine the level of 'relevant experience' you need to need to obtain a work permit. For example, if the Home Office classifies your qualification at below HND level, you will need to show at least 3 years 'relevant experience' at NVQ Level 3 or above. For example, if you are applying for a job as a Manager you must be able to demonstrate that you have relevant experience for the job at management level.

Working Conditions
Overseas workers are entitled to the same wages and conditions as people doing similar jobs, and your wage should be no lower than the National Minimum Wage.

If you are coming in to the UK to work, your employer will usually assist you in finding accommodation, although you will normally have to pay for your own rent, bills, and council tax. When you apply for your visa or entry clearance, you will need to satisfy the entry clearance officer that you have somewhere to live (*See Chapter 7*).

Entry Clearance
Although this is covered in more detail in *Chapter 7*, you should bear in mind that holding a work permit does not necessarily entitle you to enter the UK. When you receive your work permit, you will need to contact your nearest British Diplomatic Post or British Embassy, and apply for entry clearance or a visa. You must get your visa or entry clearance before you travel to the UK. Do not make the mistake of assuming that because you have a work permit you will automatically be granted entry clearance, or that this process is a mere formality.

If you are a national of Cyprus, Czech Republic, Estonia, Hungary, Latvia, Lithuania, Malta, Poland, or Slovenia, you do not need a visa or entry clearance. You should simply present your work permit to an immigration officer on arrival in the UK.

Is a work permit transferable? Your work permit is not transferable. However, you can apply for a new work permit under the same category for another employer.

H O W 2 Come to the UK to Work – Main Schemes

THE VARIOUS TYPES OF WORK PERMIT CAN BE DIVIDED INTO CATEGORIES AND SUB-CATEGORIES

Four main categories are: 1) Ordinary; 2) Multiple-entry; 3) Letters of Approval; 4) Other Schemes & Arrangements.

1. ORDINARY – TIER 1 – SHORTAGE OCCUPATIONS

AT A GLANCE:

- Government recognises various skills 'shortage' occupations
- Employer does not have to prove they cannot find a resident worker
- Work permits normally granted for Tier 1 applications

GENERAL

Tier 1 work permits, cover 'shortage' occupations – such as nursing and teaching. They are generally easier to obtain and require less documentation than Tier 2 applications, which cover 'non-shortage' occupations (see below).

The Home Office recognises various shortage occupations, where skills shortages exist in the UK. The official Home Office 'Shortage' Occupations – for example, Nursing and Dentistry – fall into this category, which means that the UK employer does not have to prove they cannot find a resident worker to fill the vacancy before being granted a work permit.

Provided both employer and employee meet the criteria, a work permit will normally be granted for a Tier 1 application.

Some shortage occupations

Nurses
Doctors
Dentists
Assistant Dentists
Opthalmologists
Occupational Therapists
Pharmacists

Railways Engineers
Power Supply Engineers
Structural Engineers
Highway Engineers
Aircraft Engineers
Communications Engineer
Teachers

Social Workers
Physical Therapists
Actuary
Veterinary Surgeons
Dietician

See *Appendices* for a full list of shortage occupations recognised by the Home Office.

1. ORDINARY – TIER 2 – NON-SHORTAGE OCCUPATIONS

> *AT A GLANCE:*
>
> ◆ Some occupations not on 'shortage' list can be considered
> ◆ Employer has to prove they can't find a suitable resident worker
> ◆ Both employer and candidate must satisfy criteria

GENERAL

Other occupations, although not on the official shortage list, can still be considered for a work permit provided they meet the criteria. The employer will have to prove that they cannot find a suitable resident worker to fill the vacancy. In other words, as long as the employer can show evidence that they cannot find a worker in the UK, and both applicant and employer can satisfy the criteria, they can apply for a work permit.

Some non-shortage occupations
Examples of Tier 2 or non-shortage occupations would include Senior Care Workers, Community Workers, Managers, Specialist Chefs, IT staff, and any other occupations which meet The Home Office work permit criteria.

Some categories of worker, for instance Senior Care Workers, although not on the official shortage list are still nevertheless in short supply in many areas of the country. The Care Industry in general has great difficulty in finding staff, and has looked to overseas workers in recent years to fill vacancies.

1. ORDINARY – TRAINING & WORK EXPERIENCE SCHEME (TWES)

AT A GLANCE:

- ◆ Allows people from outside the EEA to undertake work-based training
- ◆ Must be aged between 16 and 65
- ◆ Must be able to support yourself
- ◆ After a year on scheme, normally cannot reapply until after another year
- ◆ After more than a year, normally cannot reapply until after 24 months

---

GENERAL
The scheme allows overseas nationals to come to the UK for training towards a professional or specialist qualification, or to undertake short periods of work experience as an extra member of staff.

Qualification
To qualify, you must: hold a valid TWES work permit and be able to carry out the training or work experience it applies to; intend to leave the UK after the training or work experience; be aged between 16 and 65; not intend to take employment except as set out on the permit; and be able to support yourself and any dependants without needing any help from public funds.

A person who has held a Training and Work Experience Scheme (TWES) permit will not normally be eligible for another work permit until they have completed a period of time outside the UK.

If the person was on a TWES permit for up to 12 months, they will not normally be eligible to return for a further work permit until they have spent 12 months outside the UK. If they were on a TWES permit for over 12 months, they will not normally be eligible to return for a further work permit until they have spent 24 months outside the UK.

1. ORDINARY – OTHER
Other types of ordinary work permits come under categories such as Internships and General Agreement on Trade in Services (GATS).

2. MULTIPLE-ENTRY WORK PERMITS (MEWP)

GENERAL
The MEWP is designed for employees travelling regularly for short periods of work permit employment with the same employer

in the UK (other than Northern Ireland). It is not valid for the Training and Work Experience Scheme (TWES).

The MEWP is valid for between six months and two years for individual work permit holders. For sportspeople and groups of entertainers the maximum period is 12 months. MEWP holders do not qualify for indefinite leave to remain in the UK (in other words they cannot apply for permission to stay in the UK with no time limit). MEWP holders must support themselves and live without taking other employment or needing any help from public funds. They cannot bring their husband, wife, or dependent children with them to the UK.

3. LETTERS OF APPROVAL

GENERAL
Letters of approval are used in place of individual work permits, when a large group of people (20 or more) are travelling together.

4. OTHER SCHEMES & ARRANGEMENTS – SECTORS BASED SCHEME (SBS)

AT A GLANCE:

- Open to all non-European Union nationals aged between 18 and 30
- Low skilled jobs for Hospitality and Food Manufacturing industries
- Employer applies for the SBS Work Permit on behalf of the employee
- Non-skilled workers may apply
- You must return home after 12 months but can reapply after 2 months
- Does not normally lead to settlement
- You will not be allowed to bring dependants

GENERAL

The Sectors Based Scheme has been introduced recently to allow workers from outside the European Economic Area (EEA) to enter the United Kingdom to take short-term jobs in low skilled sectors. The scheme is open to all non-European Union nationals aged between 18 and 30.

Some Sectors Based Scheme jobs

Bar staff   Reception staff   Housekeepers
Chefs   Waiting staff   Kitchen assistants
Cleaners   Fish filleters   Room attendants
Concierge staff   Meat cutter   Mushroom processor

See *Appendices* for a list of jobs in the hospitality and food manufacturing industries for which Work Permits UK can issue a work permit.

Applying for an SBS Permit

You can only apply from outside the UK. You must first approach a UK employer who is advertising the vacancy. If the employer offers you a job, they will apply for a work permit for you. In practice, many people go through agencies supplying large numbers of staff and arranging the work permits on behalf of the employer.

Restrictions

You will only be granted a work permit for up to 12 months after which you will be expected to leave the UK. However, you may apply to return under the scheme after two months outside the UK.

You will not be allowed to stay in the UK permanently and the time spent on this scheme will not count towards gaining permanent residence in the UK (although it may be possible under the ten-year-long residence rules).

You cannot bring any dependants with you.

You can, however, change your employer during the period of your Work Permit, but you can only stay in the UK up to a total of 12 months.

Quotas

The government sets SBS quotas from time to time. There are limits placed on the number of SBS work permits issued to any single nationality for each of the sectors.

4. OTHER SCHEMES & ARRANGEMENTS – HIGHLY SKILLED MIGRANT PROGRAMME (HSMP)

AT A GLANCE:

- Highly skilled people to migrate to the UK to look for work
- Employed or self-employed work
- Points based system
- You do not need an employer to apply
- You will be allowed to come to UK for up to one year to find work
- After a year, you can apply to stay longer; must be economically active
- Can lead to settlement
- You can apply to bring your dependants

GENERAL

This innovative programme is designed to attract talented, highly skilled people to the UK to look for work or self-employment opportunities. Self-employed General Practitioners and Dentists qualified to practice in the UK may apply under the Highly Skilled Migrant Programme.

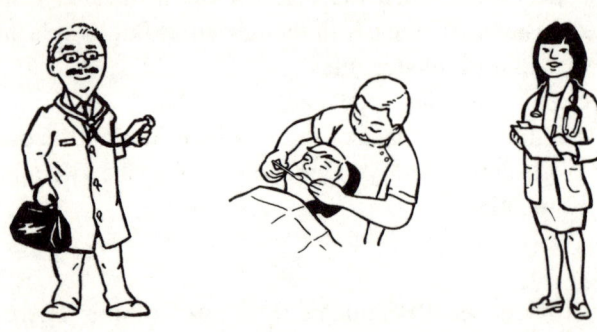

What's New?

The Highly Skilled Migrant Programme is different from the work permit scheme because you do not need a specific job offer in the UK to apply. It is different from business routes such as the Innovators scheme or other business categories because: you do not need a detailed business plan; you do not need to create jobs; and you do not need to invest in the UK.

Points Based Qualification

This is a points-based immigration scheme. Points are scored in five main areas: educational qualifications; work experience; past earnings; your achievement in your chosen field; your husband's, wife's, or unmarried partner's educational and working achievements. You need to score 65 points or more to qualify as a highly skilled migrant. The scheme has an assessment for applicants aged under 28, as well as an assessment for those 28 and over.

Maths, Science and Engineering Graduates

Graduates in maths, science, and engineering wishing to work in the UK following completion of their studies, should: have successfully completed a relevant course of a duration of one year or more, at a UK Higher Education Institution; be able to maintain and accommodate themselves without recourse to public funds; and, during their 12 months' leave, have a right, subject to meeting the various criteria, to switch in-country to Work Permit employment or the HSMP category. See *Appendices*.

MBA Provision

In April 2005, the Home Office began a scheme in which those who had completed an MBA from any of the Top 50 Management Schools after 2nd December 2004 could take advantage of MBA provision within HSMP. Ten of the Management Schools on the list prepared by the Treasury are from the UK, and 40 are from the rest of the world.

If you graduate from one of the eligible MBA programmes while that programme is on the list of eligible courses then you are eligible to apply for the MBA Provision. Successful applicants will be awarded 65 points for their eligible MBA. Like other HSMP applicants, you will also need to demonstrate that you will be able to continue your chosen career in the UK.

Although you may not have previous experience in your chosen field, you should know in what field you intend to work in the UK. You will also have to show that you intend to make the UK your main home, and that you can support yourself and any dependants without recourse to public funds.

Length of Stay

You will initially be given permission to stay in the UK for one year to seek work or self-employment opportunities. After a year, you can apply to stay for longer but you must be economically active.

If you live here continuously for 4 years with Home Office permission, you can apply near the end of the 4 years to live here permanently.

Applying
You can apply from abroad or, in some cases, from inside the UK if you are here with Home Office permission. You cannot apply if you are in the UK as a visitor, on temporary admission, or without permission, but could of course return home to apply. You may apply to the Highly Skilled Migrant Programme Team at Work Permits UK in Sheffield, or contact your Immigration Adviser (see *Chapter 8* for a list of useful websites and contact details).

4. OTHER SCHEMES & ARRANGEMENTS – THE SEASONAL AGRICULTURAL WORKERS' SCHEME (SAWS)

AT A GLANCE:

- Seasonal farm work for non EEA citizens, planting and gathering crops
- Includes processing and packing of salad vegetables, soft fruit, flowers
- Also handling livestock, e.g. lambing and on-farm poultry processing
- After more than a year, normally cannot reapply until after 24 months

---

GENERAL
The scheme allows workers from outside the European Economic Area (EEA) to enter the United Kingdom to do seasonal agricultural work for farmers and growers. In 2003-04 there were 25,000 places on the scheme. The scheme is run for the Home Office by Operators who recruit suitable people and place them on farms. The Operator may need to transfer you to other farms during your stay. To qualify for the scheme: you must live outside the European Economic Area; you must be 18 years of age or more; you must be a student in full-time education.

Applying

People who want to join the scheme must apply to the Operators. You can approach them directly, or through your university or college. The Operators give successful applicants a work card. This is like a work permit. You must then apply to your nearest British Diplomatic Post for Entry Clearance (see *Chapter 7*) before you travel to the United Kingdom. You must apply for the scheme from outside the UK.

Restrictions

You can take part in the scheme for a minimum of five weeks and a maximum of six months at a time. The Home Office expects you to leave the UK when your permission to stay is finished. You may apply for the scheme again after three months outside the UK if you continue to satisfy Home Office rules.

You can only work where the Operator places you. You can only change employer with the agreement of your Operator.

You cannot switch into work permit employment from SAWS. If you have an offer of employment in the UK, you must return home and apply at your nearest British Diplomatic post. If you want to leave the scheme, you must leave the UK. You cannot bring any dependants with you. You cannot apply to stay in the UK permanently.

4. OTHER SCHEMES & ARRANGEMENTS – INTRA-COMPANY TRANSFERS (I-CT)

AT A GLANCE:

- A work permit for the transfer of Key Staff from an overseas subsidiary
- Staff member must have been employed by subsidiary for 6 months
- Must prove a clear ownership link between companies

GENERAL

An Intra-Company Transfer work permit is for the transfer of senior or key staff into a UK subsidiary company. Multi-nationals often take advantage of this scheme.

The staff member must have been employed by the overseas subsidiary for a minimum of six months prior to an application for an intra-company transfer. The UK company must show proof of common ownership of the UK and overseas company.

WORKING HOLIDAYMAKERS

AT A GLANCE:

- ◆ For Commonwealth citizens aged between 17 and 30
- ◆ Up to 2 years
- ◆ Can work but only incidental to holiday
- ◆ Need enough money for first two months and to leave
- ◆ Cannot extend stay but can switch into work permit and other schemes

GENERAL

The working holidaymaker scheme is an arrangement whereby a Commonwealth citizen aged between 17 and 30 can come to the United Kingdom (UK) for an extended holiday for up to two years. You can work, but only provided this is incidental to the holiday. The holiday should be the primary reason for your stay.

How do I qualify as a working holidaymaker?

You qualify as a working holidaymaker if: you are a Commonwealth citizen of a country listed under the Immigration Rules, a British Dependant Territories citizen, British Overseas citizen, or a British National (Overseas); you are aged 17 to 30 years of age (inclusive); you want to come to the UK for an extended holiday, and intend to take employment as part of your holiday for no more than 12 months during your stay; you do not intend to engage in business or work as a professional sports person during your stay; you are single or are married to a person who also qualifies as a working holidaymaker and you plan to take the working holiday together; you do not have any dependent children who are aged five years or over, or who will be five before you complete your holiday; you can support and accommodate yourself in the UK without help from public funds; you have not spent time in the UK on a previous working holidaymaker visa; and you plan to leave the UK at the end of your holiday.

How long can I stay?

You can stay in the UK for up to two years as a working holidaymaker, in line with the validity of your visa. Any time you spend outside the UK during that period as part of the permitted stay will be counted and there is no provision for an extension of stay as a working holidaymaker to be granted beyond the validity of the visa on which you enter the UK.

How much work can I do?

You must intend to take work in the UK only as an incidental part of your holiday, so you must intend to spend no more than 12 months working, and to spend the rest of your stay on holiday.

What work can I do?

You can take most types of work including voluntary work, but you may not engage in any business, or provide services as a professional sportsperson. (Any other type of professional work is permitted).

When can I work?

You can choose when to work and when to take your holiday breaks as you wish, but you must not work for more than a total of 12 months or you will be breaking the conditions of your stay. *Note*: People issued with a working holidaymaker visa before 8 February 2005 do not have any restrictions upon the amount or type of work that they may do.

How much money will I need to qualify as a working holidaymaker?

You must be able to support and accommodate yourself adequately without recourse to public funds. You must be able to show that you have enough money to pay the cost of at least your outward journey. You must also be able to show that you have enough money for your accommodation and living expenses for the first 2 months after arrival, or for at least 1 month if you can show that you have arranged a job in advance which will adequately cover your accommodation and living expenses.

You should get information about how much money you will need, for example through regional tourist offices or through UK websites, for the area in which you wish to stay. This will help you find out how much you may have to spend on somewhere to stay, travel, and other basic living expenses. You will then have a clear idea of how much money you will need.

Can I apply to extend my stay once I am in the UK?

You cannot extend your stay as a working holidaymaker. But you may be eligible to switch into work permit employment after 12 months in the UK where your occupation is on the list of designated shortage occupations.

Can I switch into other arrangements?

Working Holidaymakers may also switch into Innovators and the Highly Skilled Migrant Programme (HSMP).

WORKER REGISTRATION SCHEME

From 1 May 2004, nationals of some of the new EU Accession member states working in the UK have been subject to the Worker Registration Scheme. Where they are subject to the scheme, they need to register within one month of starting work for an employer in the UK. The following nationals need to register: Czech; Estonian; Hungarian; Latvian; Lithuanian; Polish; Slovakian; Slovenian. See *Appendices*.

Forms and full instructions can be downloaded from the Home Office website: www.ind.homeoffice.gov.uk

Nationals of Malta and Cyprus working in the UK are not subject to this scheme and can apply for a residence permit now.

SPECIAL FEATURE

WORK PERMITS FOR NURSES

AT A GLANCE:

- ◆ Shortage, Tier 1, Occupation
- ◆ Need NMC Registration to practise in the UK
- ◆ Most Overseas Nurses will need 'Supervised Placement'
- ◆ Can come in on Work Permit or Student Visa

GENERAL

One of the most popular areas in overseas recruitment in recent years has been nursing. The NHS and private sector has recruited thousands of overseas nurses from countries like The Philippines, India, Africa, and Finland. The Philippine Embassy estimates that around 30,000 nurses have come to the UK in the last few years.

Nurses come under the official Shortage Occupation category, which makes it much easier to obtain a work permit. However, there are a number of requirements you will have to satisfy before you will be able to come to the UK to work as a nurse.

The Nursing and Midwifery Council (NMC) - www.nmc-uk.org

The first step is to register with 'The Nursing and Midwifery Council' (NMC). The NMC is an organisation set up by Parliament to protect the public by ensuring that nurses and midwives provide high standards of care to their patients and clients. The NMC: maintains a register of qualified nurses, midwives, and specialist community public health nurses; sets standards for education, practice and conduct; provides advice for nurses and midwives; and considers allegations of misconduct or unfitness to practise due to ill health.

The NMC has recently announced a new Overseas Nurses Programme (ONP). The full details can be found on their website, but the basis of the programme involves:

> 'A new common entry standard and 20-day period of protected learning for all nurses trained outside the European Economic Area (EEA) and, where appropriate, a period of supervised practice.
>
> Applicants whose education and practice skills need more training or education to bring them up to UK standards will, on top of the 20 days, have to do a specified period of supervised practice in a practice setting approved for the purpose. This will be for at least three months and, at most, nine months.'

The majority of nurses applying to come to the UK will require a period of supervised placement or 'adaptation' training as it used to be known, during which time they cannot practice as a qualified nurse. For instance, nurses applying to the NMC from The Philippines, India, or China will usually be issued with a letter (commonly known as a 'decision letter') stating that they will require 3 to 6 months of supervised placement before they receive their full NMC registration and are able to practice as a qualified nurse. This letter is an important document, which will not only be required before you can commence a training programme, but also when applying for a work permit and visa.

Your challenge is to find an employer or training centre which is accredited by the NMC to run the above courses in conjunction with Universities (a list of accredited employers can be found on the NMC website). Thousands of overseas nurses are applying to work in the UK, so competition is fierce!

In addition, you will have to satisfy the English Language requirements. The NMC states: 'There will first be a thorough assessment of the skills and experience of each applicant. Every applicant will have to pass the specified international English language test before they can apply to go onto the ONP.' (See *Chapter 8* for IELTS (English language testing and useful contact details).

WHICH ROUTE?

Once you have your NMC letter and job offer, there are 2 ways you can come into the UK: Work Permit; or Student Visa (see also *Chapter 3*).

Work Permit

Nurses coming to the UK to work will usually come in under a work permit applied for by the employer. The employer will have to satisfy the usual Home Office requirements to obtain the work permit.

Student Visa

Some employers choose to bring in nurses on a student visa and then apply for a work permit once the nurse is qualified following the supervised placement training. In this case you will need to apply for your visa (entry clearance) at your nearest British Embassy.

FOUR SIMPLE STEPS...
FROM JOB OFFER TO TRAVEL

STEP ONE

Job offer

STEP TWO

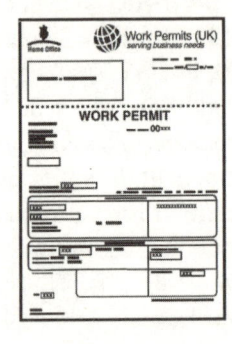

Work permit

STEP THREE

Entry clearance/Visa

STEP FOUR

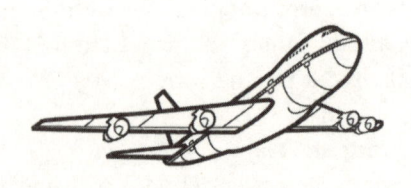

Flight to the UK

Chapter 2

H O W 2 Come to the UK for Business

BUSINESS PERSONS

AT A GLANCE:

- Nationals of European countries can do business in the UK
- Non-EEA nationals can come to the UK as Business Persons
- You need to provide a detailed business plan
- You need to show £200,000 in available funds
- Must create at least 2 full-time jobs for UK residents
- Must run the business full-time

GENERAL
The UK welcomes business people and innovators, and offers a number of schemes for those who wish to visit or settle in the UK for business purposes.

Who can come to the UK as a Business Person? Nationals of European Countries have freedom to do business in the UK subject to certain conditions. Non-European Economic Area nationals may come to the UK as business persons if they will be running a business full-time.

PLAN OF ACTION

To enter the UK as a business person you need to provide a detailed business plan. This should include: the object of the business; evidence that you have at your disposal in the UK at least £200,000 of your own money for investment in the business; evidence that you will create at least 2 full-time jobs for people already settled in the UK, and details of their employment conditions; the projected opening balance sheet following the start of the business.

If you are joining or taking over an established business, you must show audited accounts for at least 2 previous years. You also need to show that you can live in the UK without help from public funds.

You must get entry clearance as a business person before you travel to the UK. At first, you can get permission to stay for 12 months. Then you can apply for an extension of stay for up to another 3 years.

Do I have to run my business full-time?

In the UK, you can do business as: a sole trader; a partnership; or a limited company registered in the UK. As a sole trader or partner you must trade or provide services full time. As a company director, you must promote your company and manage it full-time. Self-employed doctors and dentists must practise full-time.

The full-time condition does not apply to a self-employed writer, artist, or composer.

Can I change my business? You can get permission to stay as a business person for a specific business. You must ask Home Office permission if you wish to change to a different business once you are in the UK.

SOLE REPRESENTATIVES

> *AT A GLANCE:*
>
> ◆ Will establish a wholly owned subsidiary or register a branch
> ◆ Firm must have no existing branch, subsidiary, or representative in UK
> ◆ Scheme for non-EEA nationals
> ◆ Initial permission to stay for 12 months
> ◆ Can only represent the named company

GENERAL

If you are not a European Economic Area national, you can come to the UK to act as a sole representative.

A sole representative is someone who will establish a wholly owned subsidiary or register a branch in the UK for an overseas parent company. The firm must have no branch, subsidiary or other representative in the UK. If the firm has a legal entity in the UK but this does not employ staff or transact business, then they could have a sole representative in the UK.

Restriction: You cannot do business for yourself or represent any other company's interests.

PLAN OF ACTION

You need to provide: a full description of the parent company's activities with details of assets and accounts; your job description, salary, and contract of employment.

You need to show evidence that: you have been employed by the parent company for some time and hold a senior post; you have authority to take decisions without reference to the parent company; you were recruited to the parent company outside the UK; you are directly employed by the parent company and not acting as an agent marketing the company's goods; you can live in the UK without help from public funds; you are not a majority shareholder in the parent company.

You may get entry clearance before you travel to the UK. At first, you can get permission to stay for 12 months. Then you can apply for an extension of stay for up to another 3 years.

Can I bring a colleague with me to work in the UK?
You must apply for a work permit for your colleague before bringing them to the UK.

What happens if the company's circumstances change?
If you have 2 years' permission to be in the UK, you may stay here even if your overseas company appoints a superior. You may also eventually qualify for indefinite leave to remain as long as you continue to fill a genuine vacancy, and the company wishes to retain your services. A sole representative with less than 2 years' permission to be here would need to apply for a work permit to continue working in the UK if a superior was appointed.

INVESTORS

AT A GLANCE:

- Must have at least £1 million to invest in the UK
- Must intend to make the UK your main home
- You must have a plan of what you're going to invest in
- Can't make certain investments, such as property companies
- Dependants can come to UK and work

GENERAL
This category is for people who have at least £1 million to invest in the UK, and who want to make the UK their main home. There are restrictions on the investments you can make if you come to the UK as an investor.

Can I come as a visitor rather than to live?
If you do not wish to come to the UK in the investor category, you can invest your money exactly as you please and can spend time here as a visitor for up to six months at a time.

PLAN OF ACTION
You must be able to show that you are going to make the UK your main home; you have at least £1 million which you will bring to the UK. This can either be your own money which is not held in trust, or it can be loaned money if you have a personal net worth of at least £2 million and the loan is from a financial institution regulated by the financial services authority. The calculation of your personal net worth includes illiquid assets such as property, offshore trusts, and assets held by your spouse if you are both coming to the UK.

You have a plan of your proposed investments. The plan must show that: you are going to invest at least £750,000 of your capital in United Kingdom Government bonds or in share capital or loan capital in active and trading United Kingdom registered companies other than property companies; and you can live in the UK without help from public funds or having to work as an employee.

You will need to show that you will receive enough money to support and accommodate yourself and any dependants without having to work (other than on a self-employed basis) or get help from public funds. Although £1 million would normally create a large income, the exact amount you need will depend on your circumstances. If you need to add to your investment income by earning money on a self-employed basis, you should also provide details of the work you plan to do. You can, for example, be a non-executive director or consultant, or own your own company.

You may get entry clearance before travelling to the UK. At first, you will get permission to stay 12 months. You may apply to stay longer before the end of 12 months. As to requirements, you may be allowed to stay another 3 years if you can show that: the UK is your main home; you have brought at least £1 million of money into the UK, and it is still here (can be your own money, or it can include loaned funds if you have maintained a personal net worth of at least £2 million, and the loaned funds are from a financial institution regulated by the financial services authority); you have invested £750,000 as required; and you have lived in the UK without help from public funds or working as an employee.

Can my dependants work?
Your husband or wife and dependant children can work if they have been given permission to come to the UK with you.

Do I have to transfer my capital to the UK before I apply for entry clearance?
You do not have to transfer your capital before you get entry clearance; but the entry clearance officer must be satisfied that you have enough money, that there are no restrictions on transferring the funds to the UK, and that you are going to transfer these funds.

When do I need to transfer the funds?
You are expected to transfer your funds to the UK when you have got entry clearance and entered the UK. The four-year qualifying period for settling in the UK as an investor will not start until you have invested your funds here.

Can the capital be in joint names?
The capital may be in the joint names of husband and wife if your husband or wife is coming to the UK with you as a dependant, and you both apply for entry clearance at the same time.

Do I have to make the UK my only home?
You do not need to make the UK your only home, but you should

spend more time in the UK than you do away, to continue to qualify for limited leave to remain as an investor.

What type of investment can I make?
You can invest in the following:

Unit trusts – You can invest in a regulated collective investment scheme, such as a unit trust, as long as you invest £750,000 in companies that meet the requirements of the investor rules.

Private companies – You must provide evidence of the shareholding or loans you have, in the form of legal documents that are signed by or on behalf of the company, for example, audited accounts.

What type of investment can't I make?
You cannot invest in the following:

Property companies – The Immigration Rules refer to companies whose main business is property investment. This means companies whose main function is to own or manage land or buildings. It does not include, for example, construction firms, manufacturers, or retailers who own their own premises. However, once you have invested at least £750,000, you can invest the remaining £250,000 as you want.

Offshore companies – You cannot invest in or through offshore companies. You must invest your money in the UK. However, you may invest your money in a wholly-owned subsidiary of an offshore company, although the investment must be in the form of loan capital. The subsidiary must be registered in the UK, active and trading, and directly benefit from the loan.

Banks or building societies – You cannot keep all your capital in a bank or building society. However, once you have invested at least £750,000 in the UK, as required by the investor rules, you may keep the rest of your capital in a bank or building society in the United Kingdom.

Can I re-invest my shares in different companies in the UK?
You can re-invest your shares if the new investment meets the requirements of the Immigration Rules, and you can show that you are continuing to invest in the UK.

Can my other investments or assets count towards my capital in the UK?
Once you have invested at least £750,000, the capital you have left can include investments and major durable assets in the UK, such as unmortgaged property and significant works of art. Personal belongings such as jewellery and antique furniture do not count as major assets.

Can I settle in the UK?
Yes, if you meet the requirements. See *Chapter 4*.

More information
The investor category is complex. We suggest that you consult your immigration, financial, and legal advisers before you embark on any investment schemes.

INNOVATORS

AT A GLANCE:

- For entrepreneurs with new and creative ideas
- You must have at least 5% share in the company
- No investment needed but ideas must bring 'exceptional benefits' to UK
- Need entrepreneurial and technical skills and a business plan
- Must create at least 2 full-time jobs for UK residents
- Qualifications or experience accepted as criteria
- Can stay 18 months, apply for residence and bring dependants

GENERAL

You may qualify as an Innovator if you have the relevant educational background and experience. You must show that you have: entrepreneurial ability; technical skills; and a good business plan.

The Innovator Scheme is different from other business categories for two main reasons: you do not need to invest a set amount of money; and someone else can provide you with money to set up your business. The scheme is aimed at entrepreneurs with new and creative ideas – who want to set up a business in the UK, especially in the areas of science and technology, including e-commerce – whose business proposals will lead to exceptional economic benefits for the UK.

PLAN OF ACTION

You must have a business plan which proposes to create at least two full-time jobs for people who are settled in the UK. (These can be made up from a number of part-time jobs). You must have shares in your company (you must hold, in your name, at least 5% of the shares in your company). The company must be registered in the UK. You must be able to live in the UK without help from public funds. You must be able to finance your business for the first 6 months (the money must be available or agreed in principle).

You may get entry clearance as an innovator, before you travel to the UK, although you may apply from within the UK. You cannot switch status if you are in the UK as a visitor. At first you will get permission to stay for 18 months. You may apply to stay longer before the end of 18 months. You may be allowed to stay up to 4 years subject to satisfying the requirements.

Your husband or wife, and dependent children under 18, may apply to come with you or join you.

How is my application assessed?
Your application will be assessed with a points system. You need to score a minimum number of points in each of three different areas, and reach an overall score. The individual scoring areas are as follows:

Personal – Work and business experience. Proven entrepreneurial ability. Educational qualifications (mainly in technology, science, and business). Personal references.

Business plan: general – Evidence that your business plan is realistic; you must show technical, commercial, and financial planning; and plans for creating a management team.

Business plan: economic benefits – What skilled jobs will you create? How many jobs will you create? What new and creative proposals will you make (for example, will you introduce a new technology, process, or product to the UK?) How much will you spend on research and development?

How long will it take to process my application?
The Home Office will normally give a decision within two weeks of receiving an application.

EC ASSOCIATION AGREEMENT

AT A GLANCE:

- ◆ You must intend to be only self-employed
- ◆ You must not do any work outside of the business
- ◆ A detailed business plan is required
- ◆ No requirement to invest £200,000
- ◆ You are not required to create any UK jobs

GENERAL

If you are a national of Bulgaria, the Czech Republic, Estonia, Hungary, Latvia, Lithuania, Poland, Slovakia, or Romania you can come to the UK to set up a company, partnership, or act as a sole trader under this agreement.

If you are a national of Slovenia you can set up a company in the UK under this agreement.

PLAN OF ACTION

You are not required to invest £200,000 or to create any UK jobs, but you must present a full business plan. You must be able to live without help from public funds. You must intend to be only self-employed and not to do any work outside of the business.

SPECIAL ARRANGEMENTS

There are special rules for self-employed business people from Turkey, Romania, and Bulgaria. Ask your Immigration Adviser.

Chapter 3

H O W 2 Come to the UK to Study

OVERSEAS STUDENTS

> *AT A GLANCE:*
>
> ◆ Can pursue a short-term course, degree, or postgraduate studies
> ◆ Must be full-time course
> ◆ Educational establishment must be on DfES Register
> ◆ Must be able to pay for course and live in UK without working
> ◆ Graduates may be able to extend stay
> ◆ Course graduates can generally take up work permit employment

GENERAL

British Education is known all around the world for its quality, and a degree from the UK is internationally recognised. The UK welcomes overseas students and is one of the most culturally diverse countries in the world with more than 100 ethnic groups. For students registering on courses which last more than six months, they have free access to the National Health Service (NHS).

The UK currently has thousands of people studying at more than 170 universities, 500 further education and specialist colleges, and other accredited institutions. There are more than 300,000 international students from more than 180 countries in the UK currently, and the British Council believes this could rise to more than 800,000 by the year 2018.

A number of specific categories of student are included in the immigration rules. Students may wish to remain in the UK or return after their formal studies are over to continue to write up a PhD thesis after the formal period of study has ended, or re-sit an exam without attending classes. There is also now provision in the rules for students' union sabbatical officers.

Always remember that the three most important requirements for admission into an educational institution in the UK are: a strong academic background; good command of the English Language; adequate financial resources.

PLAN OF ACTION

The application procedure for education in the UK is a lengthy one. You should begin the application process no later than a year before, for admission to the following year.

Decide on your field of study, and establish your goal: is it a certificate / diploma / degree course?; and does it satisfy your future goals? Make a list of preferred courses. Take English tests: e.g. IELTS, TOEFL. Is there a future demand for professionals in your chosen field? Can studying in the UK enhance your career? Find out the exact amount of tuition fees, cost of accommodation, deposits, and other fees so as to set out your budget.

When applying for entry clearance, you must be able to show that you have been accepted on a course of study at an educational establishment that is on the UK's Department for Education and Skills (DfES) Register of Education and Training Providers. Contact and website details for the DfES are in *Chapter 8*.

The UK educational establishment could be a school, English language institution, vocational institution, or higher education institution.

You must be able to show that you are going to follow: a

recognised full-time degree course; or a course run during the week involving at least 15 hours of organised daytime study each week; or a full-time course at an independent fee paying school.

You must also be able to pay for your course, and support yourself and any dependants, and live in the UK without working or any help from public funds; and intend to leave the UK when you complete your studies.

Academic requirements are set by the individual institutions, and hence exact requirements vary from one institution to another, and from one course to another. The standard length and content of the qualifications you have completed will be taken into account.

When submitting an application to register for a course, enclose a letter explaining your institution's grading / ranking system, and a copy of your course syllabus. Do not try to equate your qualification obtained overseas with that of a British qualification, just because they have the same title and duration.

If your first language is not English, you can prove that you can speak, write, and understand English well, through a variety of ways including in the form of test score results such as International English Language Testing System (IELTS) and Test of English as a Foreign Language (TOEFL). See *Chapter 8* for more on The British Council and Association of English Language Schools (ARELS).

Postgraduate Studies

British Masters Degrees are highly valued because they give a detailed and professional understanding of the subject, and also because they are intensive and can generally be completed in a year. Moreover, a high proportion of Masters Degrees are vocational, leading towards specific careers.

An MA student on a year-long Masters programme cannot work full-time until after they have handed in their dissertation. After you have submitted your dissertation, you can work full-time for a maximum of four months.

You need to apply for entry clearance before travelling to the UK.

STUDENT NURSES

AT A GLANCE:

- ◆ Must show acceptance for training as student nurse or midwife
- ◆ Or already qualified abroad and enrolled on adaptation course
- ◆ Must not intend to do other work, and be self-supporting
- ◆ Can enter as prospective students, for interview or to arrange training
- ◆ Spouses and children admissible on same terms as other students
- ◆ Must have been assessed by the Nursing & Midwifery Council

GENERAL

Nursing students have to show: they have been accepted for training as a student nurse or midwife (leading to a recognised British qualification), or are already qualified abroad and are enrolled on an adaptation course leading to registration in the UK under the Central Council for Nursing, Midwifery and Health Visiting; they are able to, and intend to follow the course of training; they do not intend to work or engage in business other than their nursing training; and they have sufficient funds for accommodation and maintenance in the UK without using public funds – this can include funding from a Department of Health bursary.

People wishing to train as nurses may also enter as prospective students, in order to come for interviews at hospitals, and to finalise arrangements for their training. Visa nationals (see *Appendices* for list) are not able to change status within the UK to become student nurses; they must have entered with a student nurse or prospective student entry clearance. The spouses and children of student nurses are admissible on the same terms as those of other students.

Nurses from non-EEA countries may apply to switch into work permit employment after qualification, without leaving the UK, provided they satisfy the work permits criteria and have existing leave as a student nurse.

OVERSEAS DOCTORS VISITING TO TAKE PROFESSIONAL AND LINGUISTIC ASSESSMENT BOARD (PLAB) TESTS

Although some doctors and dentists who qualify overseas are entitled to full registration with the General Medical Council (GMC) of the UK, most are required to pass an assessment test first. This test is set by the Professional and Linguistic Assessment Board (PLAB) to assess medical expertise and knowledge of English. An applicant seeking entry to take this test should produce a letter from the GMC, or a test admission card.

You may be admitted for six months with a possibility of extension for up to 12 months. Entry Clearance Officers must be satisfied that, if an applicant fails a PLAB test, they will leave the UK.

After passing a PLAB test, limited registration with the GMC is given. If successful, applicants may switch category to that of Postgraduate Doctor.

POSTGRADUATE DENTIST, POSTGRADUATE DOCTOR

> *AT A GLANCE:*
>
> ◆ Must qualify under GMC or GDC rules
> ◆ Must intend to do training in hospital or Community Health Services
> ◆ There are restrictions on how long you can spend in posts
> ◆ Must intend to leave UK at end of stay
> ◆ Must be self-supporting
> ◆ Spouses and children admissible on same terms as other students

GENERAL

Postgraduate doctors and dentists who want to study and gain experience in the UK have to satisfy the following rules: applicants must either be graduates of UK medical schools intending to do their pre-registration house officer jobs for up to 12 months, or be eligible for provisional or limited registration with the General Medical Council or General Dental Council and intend to undergo postgraduate training in a hospital or the Community Health Services; applicants cannot spend more than one year as pre-registration house officers nor more than four years, in aggregate, in posts at Senior House Officer or equivalent level, and they must intend to leave the UK at the end of their training period – they will normally be admitted for 12 months initially, and may be granted yearly extensions up to a maximum of three years; and they must show that they can maintain and accommodate themselves and any dependants without using public funds.

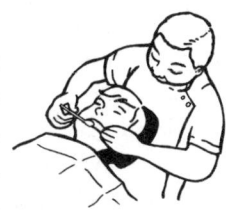

Their spouses and children are eligible for entry on the same terms as those of other students.

RE-SITTING STUDENTS

> *AT A GLANCE:*
>
> ◆ Must meet all requirements for admission as students
> ◆ Or, if no longer on full-time course, there are other requirements
> ◆ Spouses and children admissible on same terms as other students

GENERAL

Students who wish to enter to re-sit examinations have to meet all the requirements for admission as students (see above).

Alternatively, if they are no longer actually enrolled full-time on a course and attending classes, they must show that they met all the requirements of admission as students in the previous academic year, and that they continue to meet the following requirements: they intend to leave the UK at the end of their studies; they do not intend to engage in business or take employment except authorised part-time or vacation work; they are able to meet the costs of their course without recourse to public funds; they must produce written confirmation from the educational institution or independent fee-paying school that they do attend, or did attend in the previous academic year, and that they are required to re-sit the examination; they must provide satisfactory evidence of regular attendance during any course which has already begun, or any course which they attended in the past; they must, if they have been studying with a government or international scholarship agency sponsorship which has come to an end, obtain the written consent of their official sponsor for a further period of study, and provide evidence that sufficient sponsorship funding is available; and they must show that they have not previously been granted leave to re-sit their examination.

People who seek leave to remain to re-sit examinations are required to show that they were admitted on student entry clearances, if they are visa nationals.

The spouses and children of those re-sitting examinations are admissible on the same terms as those of other students. Leave will be granted to cover the period of the first available re-sit.

WRITING UP A THESIS

AT A GLANCE:

- Must meet all requirements for admission as students
- Or, if no longer on full-time course, there are other requirements
- Spouses and children admissible on same terms as other students
- May be admitted for 12 months but not to take up employment

GENERAL

Students who wish to enter to write up a thesis have to meet all the requirements for students (see above).

Alternatively, if they are no longer actually enrolled full-time on a course and attending classes (note that most research students don't 'attend classes'), they must show that they met all the requirements for admission as students in the previous academic year, and continue to meet the following requirements: they intend to leave the UK at the end of their studies; they do not intend to engage in business or take employment except part-time or vacation work; they are able to meet the costs of their course, and to maintain and accommodate themselves and any dependants without using public funds; they must demonstrate that they are a postgraduate student enrolled in an educational institution as either a full-time, part-time, or writing-up student, and demonstrate that their application is supported by the educational institution; if they have been studying with a government or international scholarship agency sponsorship which has come to an end, obtain the written consent of their official sponsor for a further period of study, and provide evidence that sufficient sponsorship funding is available; and they must show they have not previously been granted leave to write up the same thesis.

PLAN OF ACTION
You may apply for a visa for a period of 12 months. A further 12-month period may be granted if the institution can explain why a student could not complete the thesis, for example, due to prolonged illness or where the thesis submitted needs to be rewritten because it has not reached the required standard. A letter from the university will be required.

If a student is already in the UK and seeks to extend their leave to write up a thesis, then they have to additionally demonstrate that they were originally admitted on a valid student entry clearance if they are a visa national (see *Appendices* for list).

The spouses and children of those re-sitting examinations or writing up theses are admissible on the same terms as those of other students.

STUDENTS UNION SABBATICAL OFFICERS

AT A GLANCE:

- Paid full-time workers, elected by students' union, normally for 1 year
- Similar entry requirements to re-sit or write-up students
- Leave normally granted for 12 months, up to a maximum of 2 years
- No provision for the admission of dependants

GENERAL

Sabbatical officers are elected by their unions normally for one year, and are paid, full-time workers. The requirements for entry or an extension of leave are similar to those who are seeking to re-sit their examinations or write up theses in that they currently are or were students in the previous academic year, can maintain and accommodate themselves, and intend to leave the UK on completion of studies which may be resumed. Leave will normally be granted for a period of 12 months up to a maximum of two years.

Unlike other students, there is no provision in the immigration rules for the admission of the dependants of students' union sabbatical officers.

EEA STUDENTS

AT A GLANCE:

- Most EEA nationals not subject to immigration law and rules
- Normally don't require leave to enter and are free to travel, work, etc.
- 2 categories: those qualifying as students; those who qualify as workers
- First category has right of residence for period of study
- Second category has more extensive right of residence

GENERAL

Most EEA nationals are not subject to immigration law and rules, but to European Community legislation. This means that they do not require leave to enter the UK, and are free to travel between EEA countries to exercise their free movement rights. They may move in order to work, to seek work, to do business, be self-employed, or to provide or receive services. Similarly, EEA nationals who are non-economically active can move between EEA countries subject to them having sufficient funds to maintain and accommodate themselves. EEA nationals are able to obtain 'residence permits', which confirm their right to live in a particular EEA country.

There are two categories of EEA nationals which may have rights as students in the UK.

In the first category are those who qualify under the specific directive on students. This provides for free movement of students: enrolled at recognised educational establishments for the principal purpose of following vocational courses (in practice this probably means all courses); who have declared that they have sufficient resources to avoid needing to use public funds; and who are covered by all-risk sickness insurance.

These students have a right of residence for the period of their studies, and are entitled to residence permits if they apply for them. Their spouses and children, of whatever nationality, can also stay for this period. EEA students' earnings or potential earnings can be considered to show that they will be able to support themselves. As EEA nationals, they are also free to work without needing separate permission.

In the second category are those who have established – and can retain – status as workers. These are EEA nationals who have worked in the UK before studying. As well as the rights pertaining to free movement of workers, they may retain the more extensive right of residence which goes with that status. This has advantages for family members who will be able to work without restriction.

Students who are no longer actually working will retain their status as workers if they: have been in employment since last entering the UK (but not simply in order to qualify for a grant); and were engaged in economic activity which was not marginal or ancillary, but 'genuine and effective'; and intend to study on a vocational course related to their previous employment in the UK or, in the case of involuntary unemployment, intend to transfer to a new employment sector.

Students who work part-time whilst studying, provided the work is not marginal or ancillary, may argue that they are exercising their right to work, and will fall within this category as workers anyway.

WORKING WHILST STUDYING

AT A GLANCE:

- ◆ You can take a part-time job to make life more comfortable
- ◆ Depending on status, you may need to register / get permission
- ◆ Depending on stamp in passport, you may be able to work 20 hrs / wk
- ◆ Placements and internships are not restricted to 20 hours rule
- ◆ You may be able to change a 'prohibition' in your passport

GENERAL

The rules say that you must be able to support yourself financially while studying in the UK, without being dependent on money earned from taking a part-time job. However, if you do take a part-time job, the money that you earn will obviously make your life in the UK more comfortable.

Working in the UK will also give you the chance to practice your English and develop a number of transferable skills, thereby increasing your chances of finding employment, either in the

UK or in your own country. You will also have the chance to learn more about local, national, and other cultures, and make new friendships.

Students from Switzerland, an EU, or EEA country do not need permission to work in the UK.

With the exception of Malta and Cyprus, students from the new EU accession countries that joined the EU on 1 May 2004 (Czech Republic, Hungary, Poland, Estonia, Latvia, Lithuania, Slovenia, Slovakia) must apply for a registration certificate if they want to work in the UK.

Details of the Worker Registration Scheme (WRS) can be found on the Home Office's website: www.workingintheuk.gov.uk. See *Appendices*.

For international students from outside the EU, EEA, and Switzerland, check your passport. The stamp that you have been given may allow you to work within certain 'restrictions' or prohibit you from working.

If you have either of the following 2 stamps in your passport you are allowed to work up to a total of 20 hours per week during term-time and any number of hours during vacations. There is no need to seek authorisation from a government department.

Student stamp A	Student stamp B
Leave to enter the United Kingdom on condition that the holder maintains and accommodates himself and any dependants without recourse to public funds and does not enter or change employment paid or unpaid without the consent of the Secretary of State for Employment and does not engage in business or profession without the consent of the Secretary of State for the Home Department is hereby given for/until...............	No recourse to Public funds Work and any changes must be authorised

What if I am on a Sandwich course / Internship?
If you have one of the above student stamps you have permission to complete placements which are part of a 'sandwich course' and also 'internships'. Placements and internships are not restricted by the 20 hours per week rule.

Is my dependant (my spouse or child) allowed to work?
Your dependants will be allowed to work if they receive the passport stamp or sticker that allows them to work. If they have the correct stamp that does NOT say that they must not work or enter into employment, then they are free to work full-time.

Does my post-graduate programme allow me to work full-time during my vacation?
An MA student on a year-long Masters programme cannot work full time until after they have handed in their dissertation. After you have submitted your dissertation, you can work full-time for a maximum of four months.

If my passport appears to say that I am prohibited from working, can this be changed?
If you have either of the following two forms of words in your passport, then you are not allowed to work.

'No work or recourse to public funds'

'Leave to enter the United Kingdom on condition that the holder maintains and accommodates himself and any dependants without recourse to public funds, does not enter employment paid or unpaid and does not engage in any business or profession, is hereby given for/until ....'

If you are prohibited from working, we suggest you contact a registered Immigration Adviser to seek further advice.

SWITCHING TO WORKER STATUS

> *AT A GLANCE:*
>
> ◆ It is possible to switch from student to work permit status
> ◆ Must meet various conditions
> ◆ Academic Visitors can no longer switch

GENERAL

You may switch from student to work permit holder employment provided you meet these conditions: you have completed a recognised degree course in the UK – this must be at a publicly funded further or higher education institution or a bona fide private education institution; the institution must maintain satisfactory records of enrolment and attendance; you hold a work permit for employment; if sponsored by a government or international scholarship agency, you must have their written consent.

Switching by student nurses and postgraduate doctors and dentists. The Home Office normally accepts applications to switch where a student nurse or postgraduate doctor or dentist meets these two conditions: he or she must hold a work permit for employment as a nurse, doctor, or dentist; if sponsored by a government or international scholarship agency, he or she must have their written consent.

Switching by academic visitors

A person who obtains leave to enter or remain in the UK as an academic visitor can no longer change ('switch') immigration status whilst in the UK into work permit employment.

Individuals seeking entry to the UK for the purposes of sponsored research from 9 May 2005 should seek to do so as work permit holders under the 'sponsored researcher' category.

However, individuals who obtained leave to enter or remain in the UK under the sponsored researcher provisions of the Academic Visitor Concession before its revision (i.e. prior to 9 May 2005), may be permitted to 'switch' into work permit employment for the purposes of sponsored research. This is provided the work permit application meets the requirements of the work permit arrangements.

WORKING AFTER YOUR STUDIES IN THE UK

AT A GLANCE:

- Most graduates from outside EEA need a work permit
- Need to find an employer willing to obtain one for you
- Some science and engineering graduates do not need a work permit
- There are various schemes, see relevant websites

GENERAL

If you are a student from outside the EEA, you will need to find an employer willing to obtain a work permit for you. This is not as simple for the employer as if they employed someone from inside the EEA, since to obtain a work permit adds administration and cost to the recruitment process.

However, it is often simply the case that employers are put off applying for a work permit because they do not know how to go about it. Therefore, it is a good idea to ask your Immigration Adviser, Careers Service, or International Office if they have an information sheet for employers that you can take to interview.

If you graduate in an approved science or engineering subject you can apply to stay in the UK, to look for or to take work, for an additional year after your degree course finishes without getting a work permit. Also see *Chapter 6*.

I had a student visa but I have finished my programme and have sent my visa off to be renewed as a 'visitor'. Can I continue to work until the Home Office sends my visa back?
Yes – student conditions are applicable until the new visa comes back. You must stop work immediately when the visa returns (if you are granted a 'visitors' visa).

Finding a job is hard work... so here are some TIPS: d*o your research; ask for help and advice from a Recruitment Adviser, Careers Service, and International Office; perfect all your documentation – check your English; contact as many companies as you can; be positive, imaginative, and patient!*

Schemes for working after studying

There are a variety of schemes open to international students from outside the UK. They change frequently. Check the UKCOSA and Home Office websites (see *Chapter 8 – Useful Websites*) for updated information. Please tell your Immigration Adviser, Careers Service, or International Office of any new schemes you hear about so they can investigate their validity.

Check to see whether your university or other learning institution is organising any workshops for international students about the opportunities to work after study.

Students sponsored by government or international sponsorship agencies should seek advice from an immigration specialist as the application process will be more complicated.

The following tables summarise the schemes available:

Science and Engineering Graduate Scheme (SEGS)

Permission to stay	For up to one year after completing studies.
Who can apply?	Certain UK science, mathematics, engineering, and technology graduates with a 2.2 or higher (see Home Office website for list of JACS codes).
Restrictions on type of work / any special criteria	No restrictions. Applicant does not have to have prior offer of employment.
Further opportunities	Can switch into work permit employment / apply for the Highly Skilled Migrant Programme / switch to Innovators Scheme without leaving the UK.
Employer or student	Student

Work permits

Permission to stay	Up to five years.
Who can apply?	Anybody who can find an employer willing to secure them a work permit. Students can switch to work permit status without leaving the UK.
Restrictions on type of work / any special criteria	Easier for students wishing to work in 'Shortage occupations' (see Home Office website for up-to-date list). More difficult for non-shortage occupations when the employer must fulfil a number of requirements designed to give preference to candidates from the EEA.
Further opportunities	Applicant must have prior offer of employment (as employer applies for the work permit on their behalf). Can apply for the Highly Skilled Migrant Programme / switch to Innovators Scheme without leaving UK. Settlement after four years.
Employer or student	Employer

Training and Work Experience Scheme (TWES) permit

Permission to stay	For a professional qualification, permits are issued for the average time expected to complete the training, up to a period of 5 years. For work experience, permits are usually issued for up to 12 months, and extensions may be granted for up to a maximum of 24 months.
Who can apply?	Students wanting a defined period of work-based training, a professional qualification or some work experience.
Restrictions on type of work / any special criteria	Among other specifications (see website for further details) the student must be additional to the employer's normal staffing requirements.
Further opportunities	When TWES permit finishes, student must spend certain amount of time outside the UK. Cannot switch to work permit. Does not lead to settlement.
Employer or student	Employer

Highly Skilled Migrant Programme (HSMP)

Permission to stay	Given permission to stay for one year initially. Can then apply to extend if economically active.
Who can apply?	Individuals with exceptional skills and experience. Depends on number of 'points' student can score based on age, qualifications, work experience, past earning, achievement, and particular skills.
Restrictions on type of work / any special criteria	Applicant does not have to have prior offer of employment but must find employer within one year.
Further opportunities	Can switch into work permit employment / Innovators Scheme without leaving the UK. Settlement after four years.
Employer or student	Student

Fresh Talent Scheme - Scotland

Permission to stay	Two years.
Who can apply?	Students who have successfully completed an HND, degree course, Masters, or PhD at a Scottish Institution.
Restrictions on type of work / any special criteria	Must remain in Scotland.
Further opportunities	Can switch into work permit employment / Innovators Scheme without leaving the UK. Does not lead to settlement.
Employer or student	Student

Innovators Scheme

Permission to stay	Up to 18 months. Can apply to extend after 18 months usually up to a maximum of four years.
Who can apply?	Entrepreneurs who wish to establish businesses without the need to invest large sums of money. Aimed mainly at entrepreneurs in areas of science and technology, including e-commerce.
Restrictions on type of work / any special criteria	For specifications please see website: www.workingintheuk.gov.uk
Further opportunities	Can apply to stay in UK permanently after four years.
Employer or student	Student

Note: if you want to stay on in the UK under one of the above schemes, you must make your application before your current permission to be in the UK as a student runs out.

Other opportunities available to non-EEA students:

Voluntary workers
You can apply to remain in the UK for up to 12 months as a voluntary worker if: the work is for a registered charity of recognised body; it involves direct assistance to those the charitable organisation has been established to help; it is unpaid. You must intend to leave the UK at the end of your stay.

UK Ancestry
This is for commonwealth citizens who: are aged 17 or over; can prove they have a grandparent who was born in the UK, Channel Islands, or the Isle of Man. Applicants must intend to take or seek employment in the UK. If they are eligible, they will be granted up to four years' permission.

Working Holidaymakers
Applicants will need to leave the UK to apply for entry clearance. It is advisable that you go back to your home country to do this. The maximum period of time allowed on a working holidaymaker visa is up to two years.

There is further information about specific areas of work, such as the Japan Youth Exchange Scheme (see *Chapter 6*) and EU Association Agreements, on the Home Office website.

For other schemes and programmes, visit the website: www.workingintheuk.gov.uk or contact your Immigration Adviser.

Application process
The length of time needed to apply for one of the above schemes varies. For up-to-date information, ask your Immigration Adviser or check the Home Office website.

Chapter 4

H O W 2 Come to the UK to Settle

PARTNER, HUSBAND, WIFE, FIANCÉ OR FIANCÉE

AT A GLANCE:

- Your partner must be settled or coming to settle in the UK
- Couple needs to be self-supporting and have suitable accommodation
- Both partners need to be over 18
- Only one partner can join the partner already here
- Married: initial 2 years stay, then you can apply to stay permanently
- Unmarried Partners: same stay rules as married if can prove relationship
- Fiancé(e): initial 6 months, if then marry, can apply for 2-year extension
- Must get a visa before travelling to the UK

GENERAL

There are various arrangements in place for you to come to the UK as the husband, wife, fiancé, fiancée or unmarried partner of someone who is coming to live permanently in the UK or is already settled in the UK.

If you want to come to the UK as the husband, wife, or unmarried partner of someone who is not settled in the UK – for example a work permit holder – you may be able to apply as a dependant.

In most cases, you will need to get entry clearance before travelling to the UK.

PLAN OF ACTION

You can apply to join your partner, husband, wife, fiancé or fiancée in the UK as long as: they currently live and are settled in the UK; or they are coming to live permanently in the UK.

You must show that: you are legally married to each other; your husband or wife is present and settled in the UK (see below); you both intend to live together permanently as husband and wife; you have met each other before; together you can support yourselves and dependants without any help from public funds; you have suitable accommodation, which is owned or lived in only by you and your household, and is a place where you and your dependants can live without help from public funds; your husband or wife is not under 18; and you are not under 18.

If your husband or wife has more than one wife or husband, only one will be allowed to join them in the UK.

At first, you will be allowed to stay and work in the UK for two years. Near the end of this time, if you are still married and intend to continue living together, you can apply to stay permanently in the UK.

If you and your husband, wife, or partner have been living together outside the UK for four years or more, and have been a British citizen for four years or more, there will be no time limit to how long you can stay in the UK.

What do 'settled' and 'present and settled' mean?

'Settled' means living in the UK lawfully, with no time limit on your stay. 'Present and settled' means that the person concerned is settled in the UK and, at the time the Home Office is considering your application under the Immigration Rules, is in the UK or is coming here with you, or to join you and plans to live with you in the UK if your application is successful.

How can I join my fiancé or fiancée in the UK?

You must show that: you plan to marry within a reasonable time (usually six months); you plan to live together permanently after you are married; you have met each other before; there is somewhere for you and your dependants to live until you get married; and you and your dependants can be supported without working or claiming any help from public funds.

You will be allowed to stay in the UK for six months but without permission to work. When you are married, you can apply for a two-year extension to your visa, and, if your application is granted, you will be allowed to work. Near the end of this time, you can apply to stay in the UK permanently.

How can I join my unmarried partner in the UK?

You can apply to join your unmarried partner in the UK, as long as: your partner lives and is settled in the UK, or is coming to live permanently in the UK; and you are aged over 18 and your sponsor is aged over 18.

You and your unmarried partner must show that: any previous marriage, or similar relationship, has permanently broken down; you have been living together in a relationship similar to marriage for two years or more; you have suitable accommodation which is owned or lived in only by you and your household, and where you and your dependants can live without any help from public funds; you can support yourselves and any dependants without any help from public funds; you intend to live together permanently; your partner is not under 18; and you are not under 18.

You will also need to show evidence of a two-year relationship. This may include: documents showing joint commitments – such as bank accounts, investments, rent agreements, or mortgages; letters linking you to the same address; and official records of your address, such as your National Insurance card or health card.

At first, you will be allowed to stay and work in the UK for two years. Near the end of this time, if you are still partners and intend to continue living together, you can apply to stay permanently in the UK.

What are the entry rules for EEA nationals?
The rules for entering the UK are different if you, your husband or wife (your 'sponsor') are a national of another member state of the European Economic Area (EEA) or Switzerland. EEA members are the member states of the European Union, plus Iceland, Norway, and Liechtenstein.

Are there any special cases?
The rules are also different if you can claim British citizenship or another connection with the UK, for example through a parent or grandparent.

CHILDREN

> *AT A GLANCE:*
>
> - A parent must already live in the UK
> - Parent must be self-supporting
> - Parents must have adequate accommodation
> - Parents must show child is theirs
> - Child must be under 18, dependant and unmarried
> - Must get a visa before travelling to the UK

GENERAL

Children can apply to join parents in the UK if: the parents live in the UK legally, with no time limit on their stay, or they are applying at the same time as the child; one parent is living and settled in the UK or is applying for settlement at the same time as the child, and has had sole responsibility for looking after the child; the child's parents can support them without help from public funds; the child's parents have enough accommodation, which they own or live in, where the child can live without help from public funds; and the child is their own.

The term 'parent' includes a step-parent where the father or mother is dead, either the father or mother of an illegitimate child and, in certain circumstances, an adoptive parent.

In most cases, you will need to get entry clearance before travelling to the UK.

PLAN OF ACTION

A child can join parents in the UK if the child, or parents, show that the child: is under 18 years of age; cannot support himself/ herself financially, is not married; and is not living away from its parents.

A child cannot normally come to live in the UK if one parent is living abroad, unless the parent in the UK has sole responsibility for the child, or if there are special reasons why the child should be allowed to join the parent in the UK.

ADOPTED CHILDREN

AT A GLANCE:

- ◆ A parent must already live in the UK
- ◆ Parent must be self-supporting
- ◆ Parents must have adequate accommodation
- ◆ All the adoption rules must be satisfied
- ◆ Must get a visa before travelling to the UK

GENERAL

To bring an adopted child to the UK, you must be able to show that: you currently live and are settled in the UK legally, with no time limit on your stay; and you can support your child and provide somewhere to live without needing help from public funds.

In most cases, you will need to get entry clearance before travelling to the UK.

How can my adopted child join me in the UK?
You, or your child, must show that he or she: cannot support themselves financially, is not married, and is not living independently away from their parents; is under 18 years of age; was adopted when both parents lived together abroad or when one or the other parent was settled in the UK; has the same rights as any other child of the adoptive parents; was adopted because birth parents could not care for them and there has been a full and genuine transfer of parental responsibility; has broken all ties with their birth family; and was not adopted just to make it easier to enter the UK.

Does the adopted child need a visa?
The adopted child must get a visa before travelling to the UK.

Will a foreign adoption order be recognised in the UK?
A foreign adoption order will only be recognised in the UK if it was made in a 'designated'* country. If the adoption order was made outside the 'designated' country, the child can apply to come to the UK to be adopted through the courts.

---

* 'Designated' country is one that is included in the Adoption (Designation of Overseas Adoptions) Order 1973.

How long can my adopted child stay?
If your child was adopted in a designated country, and both you and your husband or wife are settled here, or if you alone are responsible for the child, they will normally be allowed to stay permanently in the UK from the date they arrive. If your child has not been adopted in a designated country, they will normally be allowed to stay in the UK for 12 months so that the adoption process can continue through the UK courts.

Will my adopted child automatically become a British citizen?
Your child will only become a British citizen if you adopted them through the UK courts and at least one of you (as their adoptive parents) was a British citizen when the adoption order was made.

PARENTS, GRANDPARENTS & OTHER DEPENDANT RELATIVES

AT A GLANCE:

- Widowed parents and grandparents over 65 may qualify
- Parents or grandparents travelling together, one over 65, may qualify
- People in the above categories have to prove dependence
- They also have to have no other means of support
- Children or grandchildren in UK need to prove financial viability
- Children or grandchildren in UK need to show accommodation evidence
- Other relatives may qualify if they meet the conditions
- Must get a visa before travelling to the UK

GENERAL

If you are a widowed parent or grandparent aged 65 or over, or parents or grandparents travelling together, and one of you is 65 or over, you may qualify if: you are completely or mainly financially dependant on children or grandchildren living and settled in the UK; you have no other close relatives in your own country to help you; your children or grandchildren can support you without needing help from public funds; and your children or grandchildren have enough accommodation, which they alone own or live in, where you can live without needing help from public funds.

If you are a parent or grandparent under the age of 65, you may qualify if: you are living in the most exceptional compassionate circumstances; you are completely or mainly financially dependent on children or grandchildren living and settled in the UK; you have no other close relatives in your own country to help you; your children or grandchildren can support you without needing help from public funds; and your children or grandchildren have enough accommodation, which they alone own or live in, where you can live without needing help from public funds.

If you are over 18 and have a parent settled in the UK, or if you are a sister, brother, aunt, uncle, or any other relative of a person settled in the UK, you may qualify if you meet the conditions above and you are living alone in the most exceptional compassionate circumstances.

In most cases, you will need to get entry clearance before travelling to the UK.

What if my relative has been recognised as a refugee or has been granted exceptional leave to live in the UK?

If you are the wife or husband of a person granted refugee status in the UK, you and your dependent children under 18 may qualify for 'Family reunion' if: your husband or wife has been granted full refugee status in the UK; you were married before your wife or husband left to seek asylum in the UK; and you show that you and any dependants intend to live together.

If your wife or husband has been granted refugee status in the UK, you will not need to show that they can support you and pay for your living arrangements.

Other dependant relatives (such as parents) do not qualify for 'Family reunion' but may be allowed to join their relative if there are exceptional compassionate circumstances.

If your sponsor has permission to remain exceptionally in the UK, or has been granted 'Humanitarian protection' or 'Discretionary leave to remain', you cannot normally apply to join them until they have been granted indefinite leave (permission) to remain.

What are the requirements?
As a guide, you should supply: evidence that your sponsor (the relative you are applying to join) is settled in the UK, such as a certified copy of their passport or registration certificate, recent statements or letters from your sponsor's UK employer, bank, local authority, or building society, and accommodation that you will have in the UK.

If you are applying to join your parents, you may also need to show your original birth certificate.

How long can I stay with my parents in the UK?
If both of your parents are settled in the UK, or if one parent has sole responsibility for you, the Home Office will normally allow you to stay in the UK permanently from the date that you arrive. If you travel to the UK with one or both of your parents, the Home Office will normally give you permission to stay in the UK for the same length of time as they are given (usually a year). If one or both of your parents are allowed to stay permanently in the UK, you will normally be allowed to stay permanently as well.

How long can I stay with my children, grandchildren, or other relatives in the UK?
If you have a visa for settlement to travel with, or join a relative, the Home Office will allow you to stay permanently in the UK from the date that you arrive.

INVESTORS

GENERAL
As an Investor, you can apply for permission to live in the UK permanently if: the UK has been your main home for four years; you have spent a continuous period of four years in the UK as an investor (you will not normally be refused if you have spent a short time outside the UK, but you should keep the time you are away as short as possible – if you are away for more than six months, you may get further limited leave rather than permission to live here permanently); you have kept £1 million in the UK throughout that period (this can include loaned funds where you have maintained a personal net worth of £2 million and have invested £750,000); and you have lived in the UK without help from public funds or working as an employee.

INDEFINITE LEAVE TO REMAIN / PERMANENT RESIDENCY

AT A GLANCE:

- Non-EEA nationals may apply for permanent residency
- Work Permits Holders on 4 years continuous employment may qualify
- There are rules regarding being outside the UK for long periods
- Once ILR is granted, you may take up any kind of work
- To keep status, you should treat the UK as your home

GENERAL
A non-EEA national may apply for indefinite leave to remain or permanent residency within the UK.

How long must I be in the UK before I can apply?

The following table is a brief guide to the length of time you must spend in the UK before applying for indefinite leave to remain / permanent residency:

CRITERIA	TIME NEEDED TO QUALIFY
Work Permit Holder, HSMP, Ancestry, Investor, Writer, Composer, Artist, Sole Representative, Business Person, Domestic Worker	4 years
Marriage	2 years, 1 year if the original application was approved before 1st April 2003
Unmarried Partner of a British Citizen or of anyone with any type of long-term status in the UK	2 years
Lawful stay on any basis	10 years
Unlawful stay or combination of lawful and unlawful stay	14 years

There are rules regarding being outside the UK for long periods during your qualification period. Variables include whether your stay has been lawful or unlawful – see your Immigration Adviser.

How do I apply for Permanent Residency / Indefinite Leave to Remain?

As a guide, you will need to supply: your passport and passports of any dependants; a letter from your employer confirming employment; your current work permit, police clearance, or evidence that you have not been convicted of an offence and imprisoned, or otherwise detained in another institution over the relevant period.

Once indefinite leave to remain (permanent residence) has been granted, you may remain in the UK permanently and take up any kind of work.

To keep your permanent residence status, you should consider the UK as your home, maintain ties to the UK, and not spend longer than two years outside the UK.

CITIZENSHIP (NATURALISATION)

AT A GLANCE:

- Must have been lawfully in UK for 5 years before applying
- Must have gained indefinite leave to remain (permanent residency)
- No more than 450 days away from UK during 5-year period
- No more than 90 days away during 12 months before you apply
- Once naturalised, you can apply for a British passport

GENERAL

Overseas nationals who have completed a period of employment can apply to be 'naturalised' as British citizens if they have lawfully been in the UK specified lengths of time depending on their status.

Prior to applying, the applicant should have gained 'permanent residency / indefinite leave to remain' status.

How do I apply for Naturalisation after five years in the UK?

If you are not married to a British Citizen, you will need to meet the following requirements to apply for naturalisation: you must be aged 18 or over and of sound mind; you must be of good character; you should be able to communicate in the English language (or Welsh or Scottish Gaelic) – there are exemptions to this requirement, for example if you are elderly or mentally handicapped; you should intend to live in the UK or be in Crown Service abroad (working directly for a UK Government organisation) or be employed by an international organisation of which the UK is a member; or be employed by a company or association established in the UK.

If you are not married to a UK citizen, you will need to meet the following residence requirements over the last five years: you must have been living in the UK exactly five years before the date the application reaches the Home Office; and during the five-year period you must not have been outside the United Kingdom for more than 450 days (about 15 months); and during the last 12 months of the five-year period, you must not have been outside the UK for more than 90 days; and during the last 12 months of the five-year period of your stay in the United Kingdom you must have held permanent residence / indefinite leave to remain (ILR); and you must not have been living in the United Kingdom in breach of the UK immigration rules at any time during the five-year period ending with the date that the application is received by the Home Office.

How do I apply for Naturalisation after three years in the UK as a spouse of a British Citizen?

If you are married to a British citizen, the requirements for naturalisation are very similar to those mentioned above. The main difference is that there is a shorter residency requirement of three years in the United Kingdom, as opposed to five years. The three years of the residency requirement are counted from the date your naturalisation application is received by the Home Office.

Further details on residency requirements are as follows: you must have been living in the UK at the beginning of the three-year period; and on the date that your application is received in the Home Office, you must have permanent residence / indefinite leave to remain in the UK; and during the three-year period you must not have been outside the UK for more than 270 days (approximately 9 months); and during the last 12 months of the five-year period you must not have been outside the UK for more than 90 days; and you must not have been in breach of any UK immigration rules at any time during this three-year period of residence in the UK.

Once naturalised, overseas nationals are able to apply for a British passport.

SUCCESS STORY

Araceli (pictured above with her family) came to the UK from Saudi Arabia in 2001 – through registered immigration advisers, Charles Kelly & Cynthia Barker – to do her nursing adaptation course.

Charles & Cynthia later helped Araceli apply for her husband, Arnell, to join her on a 'dependant visa' and then they helped Arnell get a job as a maintenance man at a local nursing home.

When they got themselves established and had moved into their own accommodation, Charles & Cynthia then helped them to bring their two children to the UK.

The children now attend the local primary school in Watford. Araceli is obviously overjoyed that the family is now reunited again. She said, 'I am so happy to have my family with me, and the children are settling in well at the local primary school.'

Due to hard work, good planning, and seeking help from registered advisers, Araceli's family have quickly got themselves established in the UK, buying their own car and home just outside London.

Chapter 5

H O W 2 Come to the UK as a Visitor

VISITORS

> *AT A GLANCE:*
>
> ◆ Visit must not be for more than six months
> ◆ Must intend to leave at end of visit
> ◆ You need enough money to live without working or public funds
> ◆ Visa required depending on nationality and other criteria
> ◆ Can't work, produce or sell, but can study during visit

GENERAL

Visitors to the UK come under various categories such as tourists, including cruise passengers; academics; those coming for medical treatment; those wishing to enter for marriage or to give notice of marriage (but not to stay); those attending job interviews; those visiting as a carer/childminder for a relative; those visiting relatives or friends; those visiting for religious purposes; those on business or employment-related visits including for interviews, auditions or 'trials' (but not those setting up business in the UK); parents with children at school in the UK; relatives acting as child minders; those taking examinations (but not pursuing studies); members of NATO and Commonwealth armed forces and certain other military personnel; those taking part in archaeological digs or those attending appeal hearings.

Other categories include those who qualify as working holidaymakers. *(See Chapter 1 – How 2 Come to the UK to work).*

Whether you are visiting the UK for business or social reasons, you can only stay for a maximum of six months. If you often visit the UK, you can apply for a visa that is valid for one, two, five, or ten years. You can then visit the UK as often as you like while your visa is still valid, but you can only stay for up to six months on each visit.

Restrictions
You cannot take paid or unpaid work; produce goods or provide services in the UK; or sell goods and services to members of the public.

TOURIST VISITORS

AT A GLANCE:

- Visit must not be for more than six months
- Must intend to leave at end of visit
- You need enough money to live without working or public funds
- Visa required depending on nationality and other criteria
- Can't work, produce or sell, but may study during visit

GENERAL
You must be able to show that: you want to visit the UK for no more than six months; you intend to leave the UK at the end of your visit; and you have enough money to support yourself and live in the UK without working or needing any help from public funds.

H O W 2 Come to the UK as a Visitor

As a visitor, you can: go to meetings and trade fairs, buy goods, and negotiate and complete contracts with UK businesses; go to conferences and seminars as a delegate; find out about, check the details of or examine goods; and get training as long as it is classroom-based instruction or limited to observation only.

In limited circumstances you can also enter the UK as a visitor if you are: delivering goods from abroad; a representative of a foreign company coming to service, repair or install their products; an adviser, consultant, trainer or other kind of specialist who is employed abroad either directly or under contract by the same company or group of companies; a guest speaker or expert speaker at a conference or seminar, or you are running a conference or seminar for no more than five days; or a sportsperson or entertainer for trials or auditions, or personal appearances that do not involve performances.

PLAN OF ACTION

Before travelling to the UK, you will need to apply for a visa if you: are a visa national (see *Appendices*); are stateless – you do not have a nationality; hold a non-national travel document (a travel document which does not give you the nationality of the country that issued it); or hold a passport issued by an authority that is not recognised in the United Kingdom. (See *Chapter 7* for more information about visas and entry clearance for visitors.

ACADEMIC VISITORS

> *AT A GLANCE:*
>
> ◆ Normally by invitation, for activities of an 'academic' nature
> ◆ Cannot receive salary but can receive living expenses
> ◆ Entry granted for 12 months
> ◆ Cannot switch to work permit status, apply under 'sponsored research'

GENERAL

Academic visitor status is quite different from that of work permit status. An academic visitor will not normally have obtained a post by responding to advertisements, but through invitation, the purpose of the 'academic interchange' being to broaden knowledge, experience, and contact.

In order to obtain the above status, the following conditions must be met: the work being carried out by an individual coming into the UK must be of an 'academic' nature, for example, working on a research project, lecturing etc; the individual can only work under this status for up to twelve months; the funding for the individual must be external – this can mean being funded by his/her own institution or another institution abroad, or by a UK funding body such as the Medical Research Council, Wellcome Trust etc.; the individual cannot receive a salary but can receive money as a contribution towards his/her living expenses, in the form of a studentship, bursary, or honorarium.

A person who obtains leave to enter or remain in the UK as an academic visitor can no longer change ('switch') immigration status whilst in the UK into work permit employment.

Individuals seeking entry to the UK for the purposes of sponsored research should seek to do so as work permit holders under the 'sponsored researcher' category.

PLAN OF ACTION

If the individual wanting to enter as an academic visitor meets with the above criteria, then the action required is: a letter is sent from the relevant department of the academic institution to the individual who is coming to the UK, detailing the following points: nature of work/collaboration; duration of stay; funding arrangements – from whom and how much?; arrangements made for his/her arrival – e.g. travel and accommodation; the individual then takes this letter to the nearest British Embassy, where a 'letter of consent' can be applied for, which is much like a visa; the letter of consent is then shown to immigration on arrival in the UK.

BUSINESS VISITORS

AT A GLANCE:

- Can do business directly linked to your normal work
- Cannot do work for which you would need a work permit
- Salary should be paid from abroad
- Must show you normally live and work abroad
- Can stay for 6 months

GENERAL

As a visitor, you may do business that is directly linked to your employment or business abroad. You must not do work for which you would need a work permit. You should get your salary from abroad. You may receive reasonable travel and living expenses from sources in the UK.

As a visitor you may: go to meetings, trade fairs, conferences and seminars; buy things, and negotiate contracts with UK businesses; undertake fact finding missions, check details or examine goods; and receive training through observation and classroom instruction only.

You may also enter the UK as a business visitor if you: deliver goods from abroad – for example, if you are an international lorry driver; come as a representative of a foreign IT company to install, service, or modify their product; come as a representative of a foreign machine manufacturer to install, service, or repair machinery – as part of a contract of purchase and supply, you may install machinery that is too large to be delivered in one piece; come as an adviser or consultant to a UK firm – you must be employed abroad, either directly or under contract, by the same company or group of companies that the client firm belongs to; advisers must not get involved in project management; come to give certain kinds of training – the training must be for a specific purpose, not go beyond classroom instruction, and must not be readily available anywhere else in the UK; come as a guest speaker at a conference or seminar – this must be a single or occasional event and not a commercial venture that you are part of; come to run a conference or seminar – events must last no more than five days, and be single or occasional, involving a specialist subject that attracts a wide audience, including people from outside the UK; come as an expert to talk to UK businessmen about overseas export requirements; or come as a sportsperson or entertainer for trials or auditions, or for personal appearances which do not involve performances.

If a UK company has invited you to visit the UK, you should provide a letter from the company explaining what you will be doing and the purpose of the trip. If your company or the UK company is paying for the trip, this should also be confirmed in the letter.

There is no limit to the number of times you can visit; but

you would not be expected to spend more than six months of any 12-month period in the UK.

PLAN OF ACTION

You must be able to show that: you only want to visit the country for up to six months; you plan to leave the UK at the end of your visit; you will not need help from public funds; you normally live and work abroad, and you have no plans to base yourself in the UK; and you do not plan to work, produce goods, or provide services in the UK.

If you are a visa national, you will need a visa to enter the UK.

If you are not a visa national, you must carry documents to show immigration officers why you are visiting.

As mentioned previously in this chapter, all visitors to the UK, whether they are here for business or social reasons, can only stay for six months. There is no limit to the number of times you can visit, but you would not be expected to spend more than six months of any 12-month period in the UK.

MEDICAL TREATMENT VISITORS

> *AT A GLANCE:*
>
> ♦ Visit must not be for more than 6 months
> ♦ Sufficient funds without working or public funds
> ♦ Private treatment only (not NHS)
> ♦ No danger to public health
> ♦ Must intend to leave at the end of treatment

GENERAL

A person wishing to visit for private medical treatment may be admitted for a period not exceeding six months if: satisfactory arrangements have been made for the necessary consultation or treatment at their own expense; sufficient funds are available in the UK to meet the estimated costs – and an undertaking to do so has been produced; and private rather than NHS treatment is genuinely being sought.

In the case of a person suffering a communicable disease, they must: satisfy the Medical Inspector that there is no danger to public health; and satisfy an Entry Clearance Officer that any proposed course of treatment is of finite duration; and intend to leave the UK at the end of the treatment.

You are not allowed to enter or stay in the UK to receive treatment on the National Health Service (NHS). You must make sure that you have enough medical insurance for the whole of your stay.

Note: The UK has healthcare arrangements with a number of foreign governments so that their nationals can be referred to the UK for free hospital treatment under the NHS. You can get information about these arrangements from the Department of Health website (see *Chapter 8 – Useful Websites*), or from your nearest British mission overseas with a visa service.

PLAN OF ACTION
If you are a visa national, you will need entry clearance before travelling to the UK as a medical treatment visitor. You will need to show the medical condition requiring consultation or treatment, and satisfactory arrangements for the necessary consultation or treatment at your own expense, the estimated costs of such consultation or treatment, the likely duration of your visit and availability of sufficient funds to meet the estimated costs, and your undertaking to do so.

Can I stay more than six months for medical treatment?
If you need to stay longer than six months to complete your medical treatment you can apply to the Home Office to extend your stay, once you are in the UK.

You will need to produce evidence from a registered medical practitioner of arrangements for private medical consultation or treatment and its likely duration; and, where treatment has already begun, evidence as to its progress; and show you have sufficient funds available to meet the likely costs of treatment.

STUDENT VISITORS

GENERAL
As a visitor, you may study during your stay. You can only apply to stay longer than six months if you are accepted on a course of study at degree level or above, or you entered the UK with a student or prospective student visa (for more on studying in the UK, see *Chapter 3*).

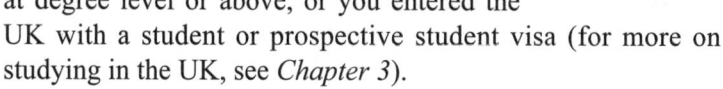

CRUISE PASSENGER / TRANSIT VISITOR

GENERAL
Visa nationals landing at a UK port in the course of a cruise and continuing their journey on the same vessel require a visa. This may be granted to a visitor in transit provided their total stay in the UK does not exceed 48 hours.

This concession is subject to certain conditions (such as a guarantee of repatriation and the presentation to the immigration authorities of a passenger list 24 hours before the ship's arrival) which the immigration authorities will bring to the attention of the agents or company who are making the arrangements in the UK. The concession does not apply to certain nationals who do not benefit from transit visa waiver.

Passengers who are visa nationals, and who intend to use a ship as a hotel and go ashore on successive days whilst it remains in port, are considered to be ordinary visitors and therefore require visit visas.

CARER VISITOR

GENERAL

There is no specific provision for carers in the immigration rules. However, a person may be granted entry clearance for up to six months to provide short-term care for a sick relative or friend or to make long-term arrangements for their care provided he/she satisfies the ordinary rules relating to visitors. It may be possible to extend the stay if the sick relative or friend is suffering from a serious illness such as cancer or AIDS, or is mentally or physically disabled. Carers cannot remain indefinitely in the UK.

MARRIAGE AND FIANCE(E) VISITORS

AT A GLANCE:

- ◆ You must give notice that you intend to get married in the UK
- ◆ Confirmation of where wedding ceremony will take place
- ◆ You will need the relevant visit-marriage visa or certificate of approval
- ◆ 70% of applications are decided within 3 weeks
- ◆ Must marry during your visit to the UK
- ◆ Fiancé(e) can leave UK after marriage and apply again as dependant

GENERAL

If you want to marry in the UK, you must either: hold a fiancé(e) or visitor-marriage entry clearance (visa); or hold a Home Office certificate of approval, or be settled in the UK (i.e. indefinite leave to remain). You must also give notice to marry to a registrar at one of a number of designated register offices throughout the UK.

These rules do not apply to British citizens, someone who has a certificate of entitlement in the passport showing right of abode in the UK, EEA nationals, Swiss nationals, other people who are not subject to immigration control because of the work they do, or anyone who has already given notice to marry to a registrar before 1 February 2005.

In addition, you must satisfy the entry clearance officer that you intend to marry during your visit to the UK.

PLAN OF ACTION

Before travelling to the UK, you must apply for a visit-marriage visa. Without this, the UK registrar will not be able to take your notice of marriage. This condition applies even if you are from a country where you would not normally require a visa to come to the UK.

If you and your fiancé(e) are both subject to immigration control, you must both apply for a visa whether you are planning a civil or religious ceremony.

In any marriage involving civil preliminaries, you will have to show your entry clearance to the registrar when you give notice of marriage. Notice must be given at one of a number of designated register offices.

If you plan to get married at an Anglican Church, you must contact a member of the clergy at the church where you plan to get married to make the appropriate arrangements. When you arrive in the UK, you should show the immigration officer evidence that you will marry in an Anglican church.

If you enter the UK as a visitor, or for another reason, for 6 months or less, you will not be able to apply for a certificate of approval. If you want to stay in the UK as your partner's dependant, you will first need to enter the UK with a visit-marriage visa. After your marriage, you must then leave the UK and return home to apply for a visa as a dependant.

How long does it take?
You should allow 3 months for your application to be decided, but 70% of applications are usually decided within 3 weeks (check Home Office service standards).

My fiancé(e) and I are both foreign nationals who currently have leave to enter/remain in visa categories other than fiancé(e), or visit-marriage. Do we require a certificate of approval for marriage?
You will both have to make individual applications for certificate of approval for marriage. All foreign nationals who wish to marry in the UK, who do not have the correct visa to do so, must obtain a certificate of approval*. This is the same, whether or not you intend to settle in the UK after the marriage.

For example: two American nationals with leave to remain as students, who want to get married in the UK, would both need to apply for a certificate of approval in order to give notice to marry in the UK to a registrar. This is the case, even though the marriage would not allow either of them to qualify for settlement in the UK.

Where can I find out more about getting married in the UK?
Information about marrying in the UK is available on the websites of the General Register Offices (see *Chapter 8*).

RELATIVES ACTING AS CHILD MINDERS

GENERAL
A person seeking entry to the UK as a temporary child minder may be treated exceptionally as a visitor if: he/she is a close relative of one of the parents e.g. brother, sister, in-law – more

---

*The Home Office certificate of approval represents the written permission of the Secretary of State to marry in the United Kingdom. The need for this written permission was introduced in the Asylum and Immigration (Treatment of Claimants) Act 2004.

distant relatives are acceptable only if they have formed part of the family unit overseas or are the closest surviving relatives of the parent; neither parent is able to supervise the daytime care of the child; it is not simply an arrangement to enable both parents to take gainful employment (i.e. the arrangement should be to help in a temporary situation only); neither parent is in a category leading to settlement; the applicant will not receive payment (except provision of board, accommodation and pocket money); the applicant intends to remain in the UK for not more than 6 months.

Child minders may qualify for entry under the Au Pair Scheme, as domestic servants, or as working holiday makers.

PERSONS COMING FOR JOB INTERVIEWS

GENERAL
An interviewee may be granted entry clearance to the UK for six months if he/she can show evidence that he/she will return to their country of origin to await the issue of a work permit and entry clearance for that purpose.

MINISTER OF RELIGION VISITORS

GENERAL
A minister of a religious order may visit the UK to attend an interview for a job as a minister of religion or visit the UK on a preaching tour. The tour must not exceed 6 months. It should involve only preaching, be consistent with the person's employment abroad and not constitute disguised employment as a minister of religion.

He or she may be able to change status in the UK ('switch') to employment as a minister of religion.

VISITORS TAKING PART IN ARCHAEOLOGICAL DIGS

GENERAL
People taking part in archaeological digs as volunteers may be granted entry clearance provided they are not paid (or receive only subsistence and travelling expenses).

PLAN OF ACTION
You should provide a letter from organising body in UK stating period of employment and, where appropriate, arrangements for accommodation and maintenance. You may stay up to a maximum of twelve months. Those employed full-time on a salary as a director of, or participant in, an excavation, require work permits.

AMATUER ENTERTAINERS & SPORTSPEOPLE

GENERAL
An amateur entertainer or sportsperson may be granted entry clearance for up to six months if he/she satisfies the requirements relating to visitors, and receives no more than board and lodging and reasonable expenses arising from his/her activity.

A professional entertainer or sportsperson may also be granted entry clearance for up to six months for activities such as personal appearances, promotions, television chat shows, publication of a book, negotiating contracts, and discussing sponsorship deals. He/she must not be employed.

APPLICANTS SEEKING RE-ADMISSION TO ATTEND APPEAL HEARINGS

GENERAL
An appellant may be granted entry clearance to the UK to attend an appeal hearing depending on the likely duration of the appeal. He/she must show evidence that he/she will leave the UK, regardless of the outcome of the appeal.

Chapter 6

H O W 2 Come to the UK – Other Schemes

PERMIT FREE EMPOYMENT

GENERAL
This a brief guide to a number of schemes and arrangements under which you can come to the UK to work without a work permit. These are generally referred to as Permit Free Employment. In most cases you will need to apply for Entry Clearance and obtain a visa at your nearest British Embassy (see *Chapter 7*). For full details on all these schemes, please check the Home Office website (see *Chapter 8 – Useful Websites*).

Permit free employment means types of work for which you do not need a work permit, such as: minister of religion, missionary or member of a religious order; sole representative of an overseas company in the UK; representatives of overseas newspapers, news agencies, and broadcasting organisations; airport-based operational ground staff of overseas-owned airlines; postgraduate doctors and dentists (for training) – including those attending Professional and Linguistic Assessment Board (PLAB) tests; teachers and language assistants coming to the UK under approved exchange schemes; seasonal agricultural workers; writers, composers and artists; overseas government employees; science and engineering graduates; and dependants of any of the above.

DOMESTIC WORKERS

> *AT A GLANCE:*
>
> ◆ You can come to the UK to work with your employer who is a visitor
> ◆ You can come to the UK to work for families of diplomats
> ◆ You can come to work for wealthy families you worked for overseas
> ◆ You can come for up to 6 months or sometimes up to 12 months
> ◆ You can apply to stay longer and, after 4 years, apply to stay indefinitely
> ◆ You may change employers within the same category

GENERAL

Domestic workers provide personal services e.g. chauffeurs, gardeners, cooks, and nannies, linked to the running of the employer's household.

You should be aged between 18 and 65. You will need to prove that you have worked as a domestic worker in the same household as your employer for one year prior to your application, or that you have been working in a household that your employer uses regularly for at least one year prior to your application. You will need to show a connection between you and your employer, your employer's husband or wife, or your employer's child (under 18). The position should be as a full-time domestic worker in the same house as your employer.

Private servants of diplomats must be at least 18 years old and must be employed full-time.

PLAN OF ACTION

You do not need to get a work permit, but you must apply for entry clearance as a domestic worker before you travel to the UK. Your employer must provide an undertaking to provide adequate maintenance and accommodation, and terms of employment in writing. You must only work as a domestic worker, and must support yourself and live without help from public funds.

Your length of stay will depend on your employer's status and intended length of stay. Check the entry clearance sticker or stamp in your passport, which gives you the date your permission to stay ends. (See *Chapter 7* for more about visas and entry clearance.)

You may change to another job as a domestic worker in a private household, and can extend your stay for periods of 12 months, but must notify the Home Office in writing outlining the reasons for the change. After four years' continuous employment as a domestic worker, you can apply for settlement in the UK indefinitely. You may bring your dependants (see *Chapter 4*). If your employer leaves the UK and you wish to stay, you should seek legal advice.

A full list of requirements are shown on the IND website (see *Chapter 8*).

VISITORS EXERCISING ACCESS RIGHTS TO A CHILD RESIDENT IN THE UK

GENERAL

The criteria for admission in this capacity are very strict, and all applications involve mandatory referrals to the Home Office.

The requirements are the same as those which all visitors need to meet except that, in addition: the applicant must be a parent of a child resident in the UK and intend to enter in order to exercise rights of access; the parent or carer with whom the child permanently resides must be resident in the UK; the child must be under 18; the applicant must have evidence that a UK court has granted rights of access to the child, or a certificate issued by a district judge confirming the applicant's intention to maintain contact with the child; the applicant must hold prior entry clearance.

You should provide as much relevant supporting documentation as possible, including evidence that you can maintain yourself and dependants; and availability of accommodation without recourse to public funds.

Leave to enter may be granted for twelve months in the first instance. If the applicant has completed a period of twelve months as a person exercising rights of access to a child, he/she may apply for settlement or indefinite leave to remain in the UK.

ENTERTAINERS

AT A GLANCE:

- Arrangements allow established entertainers to come to UK to work
- Most entertainers need work permits
- You may be able to come without a work permit
- Your dependants can come with you
- It may be better to apply as a business visitor

GENERAL

The entertainer's arrangements allow employers in this country to employ established entertainers, cultural artists, and some technical/support people from outside the EEA. An entertainer is someone who comes to the UK to perform as an amateur or professional.

Most entertainers need work permits. In some cases, you

should enter the UK as a business visitor rather than an entertainer.

Business visitors do not need work permits. Entry as a business visitor would allow you to: negotiate contracts or discuss sponsorship; perform at auditions as long as you are not being paid to do so; make personal appearances and promotions (for example, TV chat shows or interviews).

PLAN OF ACTION

There are various categories of entertainers listed on the IND website, examples include: professional entertainer coming to take part in music competition; Sikh religious entertainer; amateur entertainer seeking entry as an individual performer; amateur or professional entertainer taking part in a cultural event sponsored by a government, a recognised international organisation or a major art festival*; a professional entertainer taking part in a charity concert or show where the organisers are not making a profit, and no fee is to be paid to the entertainer.

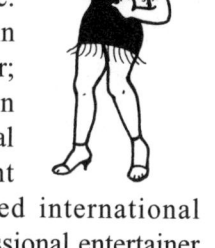

You can come to the UK as an entertainer without a work permit if you hold a genuine invitation to perform at one or more specific events. You must not use your engagement to establish yourself in the UK. You need entry clearance before you come to the UK if you are a visa national. You must not intend to stay in the UK for more than 6 months. Your husband or wife and dependant children can come with you. If they are visa nationals, they will need entry clearance. (For more information, see *Chapter 7*.)

---

*There is a festival list, updated yearly (see *Chapter 8 – Useful Websites*). Festivals can apply to be added to the list if they: have been established for more than three years; make a significant contribution to cultural life in the UK; employ a significant number of non-EEA performers; and have an expected audience of more than 10,000.

What evidence will I need to show when applying for my Visa?
You need an invitation from the UK events organiser, evidence that you can support yourself in the UK without help from public funds or working, and evidence that you can cover the cost of your trip home.

POSTGRADUATE DOCTORS AND DENTISTS

> *AT A GLANCE:*
>
> ◆ Doctors and dentists can come to do postgraduate training
> ◆ You must register with the GMC or CDC; first passing PLAB test
> ◆ Doctors need to take IELTS (English language) test before PLAB test
> ◆ If you are coming to work, you will need a work permit
> ◆ You can apply for further or indefinite leave to remain

GENERAL
You can do postgraduate training if you are a doctor or dentist who has qualified either in the UK or abroad.

How do I qualify?
In order to qualify to come to the UK for postgraduate training, you must show that: you are a doctor or dentist; you are registered, or eligible to be registered, with the General Medical Council or General Dental Council; you plan to carry out postgraduate training in a hospital or the Community Health Services (or both); you have not already spent four years in postgraduate training in the UK (this does not include the 12 months you worked as a house officer); and you plan to leave the UK when you finish your training.

Do I need to register with a professional body?
You must register with the General Medical Council or the General Dental Council before you can start postgraduate training.

Do I qualify to register with the GMC or GDC?
You qualify for full registration with the General Medical Council if you have worked as a house officer in a hospital for up to 12 months.

If you qualified abroad, you may need to pass a test set by the Professional and Linguistic Assessment Board (PLAB) before you can register with the General Medical Council. The test shows how much you know about English and medicine.

Doctors must pass an English test, known as the International English Language Testing System (IELTS), before they can take the PLAB test. You do not have to take this test in the UK. You can take it at over 100 centres around the world. The Home Office may give you permission to stay for up to 18 months in the United Kingdom so that you can pass the PLAB test.

How long can I stay?
You will need entry clearance for the United Kingdom. The Home Office will give you permission to stay in the United Kingdom for postgraduate training for up to three years at first. You can apply to stay for up to four years as long as you have a postgraduate job in basic specialist training or a similar job. If you have a job in higher specialist training, you may apply for permission to stay for longer than four years. Your stay can be extended for up to three years at a time.

You will need a work permit if you are coming to the United Kingdom for any work other than in a training post, and can apply for further leave to remain or indefinite leave to remain.

For more information, see *Chapter 8* for useful contact details.

SCIENCE AND ENGINEERING GRADUATE STUDENTS

> *AT A GLANCE:*
>
> ◆ Allows certain graduates chance to pursue a career in UK
> ◆ Graduates can switch to scheme in-country or return from abroad
> ◆ No restrictions on type of paid work you can do
> ◆ Normally one-year stay
> ◆ Dependants can join you

GENERAL

The UK is suffering from a shortage of physical science, engineering, and mathematics students at university, and skilled workers in the labour market. This could affect the UK's future growth.

In response to this, the Government announced that, from Summer 2004, foreign students at UK universities graduating from specific physical science, engineering, and mathematics courses would be permitted to stay in the UK for one year following their graduation to take up employment. Through the scheme, the government is looking to invest in the high achievers of tomorrow. There is a real demand in sectors such as research and development and financial services for maths, science, and engineering specialists.

The government hopes that this scheme will encourage overseas students to study in the UK and, following graduation, be a real asset in the work place.

The Science and Engineering Graduate Scheme (SEGS)

allows non-EEA nationals who have graduated from UK higher or further education establishments in certain physical sciences, mathematics, and engineering subjects with a 2.2 or higher to remain in the UK for 12 months after their studies in order to pursue a career. Applicants may apply for leave under the scheme if they have current leave as a student. Entry clearance is mandatory for those seeking leave to enter under the Science and Engineering Graduate Scheme.

The rules state that you should intend to leave the UK at the end of your stay, although you can switch or be granted leave to remain as a work permit holder, highly skilled migrant, business person, or innovator.

PLAN OF ACTION
You should: have successfully completed a second class honours (2.2) degree or higher, a recognised science or engineering degree course, Masters course or PhD at a UK institution of Higher or Further Education. You should also intend to work (no restrictions on type of work) during the period of leave to remain, granted under the scheme, and be able to maintain and accommodate yourself and any dependants without recourse to public funds. The Department for Education and Skills (DfES) has created a list of eligible Science and Engineering courses (see *Appendices*). Only those who have studied approved courses are eligible to apply for leave under the scheme.

Can my dependants also stay in the UK?
Spouses, unmarried partners, and children of students will be eligible to switch in line with the SEGS applicant. If they are applying from abroad, entry clearance is mandatory.

MINISTERS OF RELIGION

> *AT A GLANCE:*
>
> ◆ Religious workers with religious duties can come to the UK
> ◆ You cannot change job unless still working as a Minster of Religion
> ◆ You can apply to stay longer
> ◆ You can apply for permanent residence after 4 years
> ◆ There is an IELTS (English language) qualification

GENERAL

A minister of religion is a religious worker whose main duty is to lead a congregation in prayer and preach about their religious beliefs.

You must show that you have been working for at least one year as a minister of religion, or that you have been ordained after training for the ministry. The training must be at least one year full-time or two years part-time. You must also show that you plan to work full-time as a minister of religion in the UK, and that you will not need help from public funds.

You will need to obtain entry clearance as a minister of religion before you travel to the United Kingdom (see *Chapter 7*).

You can apply to extend your stay and to live in the UK permanently subject to certain conditions.

Ministers of religion are required to provide an International English Language Testing System (IELTS – see *Chapter 8*) certificate demonstrating their language skills at an appropriate level.

FILM CREW ON LOCATION

> *AT A GLANCE:*
>
> ◆ 'Film crew' includes people essential to production of film
> ◆ 'On location' means not in a sound stage or studio
> ◆ Should be employed / paid overseas and only coming for location work
> ◆ Permission to stay is normally 12 months
> ◆ You can apply for extension if still filming

GENERAL

A 'film crew' includes people essential to the production of the film: actors; producers; directors, and technicians. 'On location' means not in a sound stage or a studio. If this is the type of work to be done, it comes under the category of 'permit free' employment. Film crew who want to come to the UK for other work (e.g. studio work; pre- or post-production work; or if you are employed or paid in the UK) will need a work permit.

You can come to the UK as a film actor, producer, director, or technician if you are employed and paid overseas and coming only for location sequences.

PLAN OF ACTION

You must apply for entry clearance before you travel to the UK and should get permission to stay for up to 12 months. This can be granted if you still have work to do.

REPRESENTATIVES OF OVERSEAS MEDIA ORGANISATIONS

AT A GLANCE:

- Employees of overseas newspapers, news agencies etc
- Assigned to UK on long-term, full-time salaried basis.
- Employer must not be UK registered company
- Must give evidence of posting
- 12 months initially, can apply for extension and residence

GENERAL

Representatives of overseas media organisations are employees of overseas newspapers, news agencies, and broadcasting organisations assigned to the UK on a long-term, full-time, salaried basis. The category also includes correspondents employed by overseas media, producers, news cameramen, and front of camera personnel.

Representatives of overseas media organisations, correspondents employed by overseas media, producers, news cameramen, and front of camera personnel do not need work permits. You will, however, need entry clearance if you are a visa national.

Secretaries and other administrative staff do require work permits. It may be possible for staff coming for less than 6 months to enter the UK as business visitors provided that they qualify under the business visitor rules.

Your husband or wife, and dependant children, can accompany you provided they obtain an entry clearance.

OVERSEAS GOVERNMENT EMPLOYEES

AT A GLANCE:

- An employee of an overseas government or international organisation
- Must provide evidence of status
- Family can accompany as long as they get entry clearance
- 12 months initially, can apply for extension and residence

GENERAL
This is for employees of an overseas government, United Nations organisation, or other international organisation of which the UK is a member. You will initially be given permission to stay for 12 months, but this can be extended and could eventually lead to permanent residence subject to the usual rules (*see Chapter 4*). You cannot switch into this category if you are already in the UK. Your husband, wife, and dependants can accompany you.

PLAN OF ACTION
You must show that you have a valid UK entry clearance or evidence of your status as an overseas government employee; you intend to work full-time for the government or organisation concerned; you have enough money to live in the UK without working or help from public funds; you do not intend to take any other employment.

JAPAN YOUTH EXCHANGE SCHEME

AT A GLANCE:

- For Japanese nationals aged 18 to 25, 400 places per annum
- Employment restricted to incidental work
- Can come once only
- You can stay 12 months, no extensions allowed

GENERAL

This scheme allows up to 400 young Japanese nationals aged between 18 and 25 to come to the UK for an extended working holiday for up to 12 months only. Your employment is restricted to incidental work. You will need entry clearance and you can only come to the UK once under this scheme.

For full details and up-to-date information, we suggest you check the Home Office, IND website (see *Chapter 8 – Useful Websites*) before submitting an application.

SPORTSPEOPLE

> *AT A GLANCE:*
>
> - For established sportspeople to work for UK employers
> - Will need to show a genuine invitation from a UK events organiser
> - No more than 6 months
> - Might be more applicable to enter as a business visitor, e.g. for trials
> - This category covers helpers such as grooms and coaches

GENERAL

The arrangement allows employers in the UK to employ established sportspeople from outside the EEA. You must plan to stay in the UK for no more than 6 months, have a genuine invitation from the UK events organiser, show evidence that you can live in the UK without help from public funds or working, and that you can pay for your journey out of the UK. You will need entry clearance before you travel to the UK if you are a visa national.

You do not need a work permit to come to the UK as a sportsperson, but there are some sporting activities you cannot take part in. If you want to come to the UK for a holiday that involves recreational sport, you may enter as a visitor.

In some cases, you should enter the UK as a business visitor rather than a sportsperson. Entry as a business visitor would allow you to: take part in trials provided you are not paid to do so; negotiate contracts or discuss sponsorship; and make personal appearances or promotions.

As an amateur or professional sportsperson, you can participate in an event (or one-off charity sporting event), series or tournament; you can do this as an individual competitor or as a member of a team.

An amateur or professional sportsperson can join a UK club but should not receive payment.

As a groom, you can accompany a horse in a competitive event or series of events. As a personal coach, you can accompany a sportsperson for an event or series of events. You can officiate for an event or series of events.

To come to the UK for other kinds of sporting activity, you need a work permit. You will need a work permit if you intend to: base yourself in the UK for a sporting season; join or represent a British team and receive pay; give coaching (unless you are a personal coach accompanying a sportsperson for a specific event or series of events); stay more than 6 months.

There are a number of rules and schemes related to Sportspeople, and you should check the Home Office, IND website to see which category you come under.

GAP YEAR ENTRANTS FOR WORK IN SCHOOLS

> *AT A GLANCE:*
>
> - For non-EEA nationals (18 to 19) to work in schools during 'gap year'
> - Must meet the various criteria
> - Work must include direct teaching in classroom
> - Normally stay for a maximum of 12 months
> - No extensions permitted

GENERAL

Under a concession operated by the Home Office, non-EEA nationals may come to the UK to work in schools during their 'gap year' (between secondary and higher education) for a maximum of 12 months.

PLAN OF ACTION

You can apply to come to the UK as a gap year entrant if you meet these conditions: you are 18 or 19 years old; you completed secondary education less than 12 months ago; you have an unconditional offer of a place on a degree course overseas that will commence after you leave the UK; you have a written offer of employment in a teaching or teaching assistant capacity in a school in the UK for three consecutive academic terms; you intend to take this employment, and do not intend to take any other employment; you have the means to pay for your return or onward journey; you will not need help from public funds; you intend to leave the UK at the end of your stay and take up your place at university overseas.

Schools employing gap year entrants may use a variety of job titles, but the work must include direct involvement in the teaching process in the classroom. Some administrative work associated with teaching is also allowed. You need entry clearance before coming to the UK as a gap year entrant.

VOLUNTARY WORKERS FROM OVERSEAS

AT A GLANCE:

- For non-EEA nationals to come to UK to do voluntary work
- Normally 12 months at a time, can come repeatedly
- Must do fieldwork, offering direct assistance to the charity's 'clients'
- You cannot be paid
- If already in UK, you can apply to 'switch' in to this category

GENERAL

There is no provision in the Immigration Rules for non-EEA nationals to enter the UK to do voluntary work; but, to support charitable work and youth mobility, the Home Office operates a concession outside the rules.

The concession allows non-EEA nationals to come to the UK to do voluntary work subject to certain conditions, for instance that the work is completely voluntary and the activity is for a recognised organisation or registered charity. Other than pocket money, board, and accommodation, the work should be unpaid fieldwork offering direct assistance to those the charity is there to help, for example, elderly, disabled, vulnerable, or homeless people.

You can stay for a maximum of 12 months as a voluntary worker. There is no limit on the number of times you can come to the UK as a voluntary worker, but you must not plan to live permanently in the UK. You need entry clearance if you are a visa national.

Always check the Home Office, IND website for up-to-date information before submitting an application, or consult a registered immigration adviser.

FRESH TALENT: WORKING IN SCOTLAND SCHEME

> *AT A GLANCE:*
>
> ◆ For non-EEA nationals who've successfully completed Scottish courses
> ◆ You can apply whilst still in UK or to return from abroad
> ◆ Can stay up to 2 years to seek and take work
> ◆ You must be self-supporting
> ◆ Can switch to a variety of other schemes

GENERAL

The Fresh Talent: Working in Scotland scheme is part of the Scottish Executive's Fresh Talent Initiative. The Fresh Talent Initiative encourages overseas people to consider living and working in Scotland, as well as supporting efforts to retain indigenous people who wish to begin, or to further, their careers in Scotland.

The Home Office and the Scottish Executive are working together to implement the Fresh Talent: Working in Scotland scheme. This scheme will enable non-EEA nationals who have successfully completed an HND, degree course, Masters, or PhD at a Scottish university to apply to stay in Scotland for up to two years after completing their studies to seek and take work.

PLAN OF ACTION

To be granted leave under the Fresh Talent: Working in Scotland scheme you must: have successfully completed an HND, degree course, Masters course, or PhD at a Scottish institution of Higher or Further Education (the qualification must be awarded by a Scottish institution); have lived in Scotland whilst studying for your HND, degree, Masters, or PhD; intend to work during the period of leave granted under the scheme; be able to maintain and accommodate yourself and any dependants without recourse to public funds; intend to leave the UK at the end of your stay, unless granted leave as a work permit holder, highly skilled migrant, business person, or innovator.

You can only apply while you are in the UK if you have valid leave as a student (this includes leave as a student nurse, to re-sit examinations or to write up a thesis). You will not be able to switch from any other category of leave onto the Fresh Talent: Working in Scotland scheme while in the UK.

You can also apply to return from abroad under the Fresh Talent: Working in Scotland scheme up to 12 months after you complete your studies. You must have an entry clearance for the scheme if you apply from abroad. For HND and degree level students, the date you complete your studies will be the date on your graduation certificate. For Masters or PhD students, the date you complete your studies will be the date your leave as a student (or to re-sit examinations or write up a thesis) expires.

What type of work can I do under the scheme?

There are no restrictions on the type of paid work you can do if you are granted leave under the Fresh Talent: Working in Scotland scheme.

Fresh Talent: Working in Scotland scheme participants will be eligible to switch in-country into leave as a: work permit holder; Highly Skilled Migrant Programme (HSMP) participant; Business Person; Innovator. You would have to show that you meet the requirements of the category you apply to switch into. If you do not switch into one of these categories, you will have to leave the UK by the time your leave expires.

Can my dependants stay in Scotland with me?

Yes, if they meet the requirements of the Immigration Rules, your dependants will be able to stay in Scotland with you. If they are applying from abroad, they must apply for the correct entry clearance.

CITIZENS OF THE EEA AND SWITZERLAND

> *AT A GLANCE:*
>
> ◆ Citizens of the EEA and Switzerland do not need work permits
> ◆ Under EEAA, nor do citizens of Iceland, Liechtenstein and Norway

GENERAL

If you are a Swiss national, or a national of a country in the European Economic Area (EEA), you do not need permission to work in the UK.

The EEA includes these countries:

Austria	Greece	Malta
Belgium	Hungary	Netherlands
Cyprus	Iceland	Norway
Czech Republic	Ireland	Poland
Denmark	Italy	Portugal
Estonia	Latvia	Slovakia
Finland	Liechtenstein	Slovenia
France	Lithuania	Spain
Germany	Luxembourg	Sweden

From 1 June 2002, Swiss nationals have had the same rights as EEA nationals within the UK. They can work without a work permit. Iceland, Liechtenstein, and Norway are not members of the European Union (EU). However, the European Economic Area Agreement gives nationals of these countries the same rights to enter, live in, and work in the UK as EU citizens.

THE WORKER REGISTRATION SCHEME

> *AT A GLANCE:*
>
> ◆ Workers from certain new EU member states must register
> ◆ You should register as soon as you start a new job
> ◆ If you don't apply within 1 month, you will be working illegally
> ◆ There are full free movement rights after 12 months

GENERAL

Since 1 May 2004, nationals from new member states have been free to come to the UK. Nationals from the following new member states – Poland, Lithuania, Estonia, Latvia, Slovenia, Slovakia, Hungary, and the Czech Republic – who find a job in the UK are required to apply to register with the Home Office under the new 'Worker Registration Scheme' as soon as they find work. There is a small Home Office charge to obtain a certificate and a photo registration card.

Nationals from Malta and Cyprus have full free movement rights and are not required to obtain a workers registration certificate.

PLAN OF ACTION

You should apply to register with the Worker Registration Scheme as soon as you start a new job. If you do not apply within one month of starting a job, your employment will be illegal after that date.

You can change jobs, but must apply for a registration certificate under the Worker Registration Scheme authorising you to work for your new employer.

Once you have been working legally in the UK for 12 months, without interruption, you will have full free movement rights, and will no longer need to register on the Worker Registration Scheme. You can get an EEA residence permit confirming your right to live in the UK under European Community law.

If you have already registered on the Worker Registration Scheme, and have been working continuously (check website for full definition) in the UK for 12 months, you can apply for a residence permit.

Some workers are not required to register, such as the self-employed or those who had been working legally in the UK for at least 12 months on 1 May 2004.

You can register by going to: www.workingintheuk.gov.uk or consult a registered immigration adviser.

AU PAIRS

AT A GLANCE:

- For single people between 17 and 27 to come to UK to study English
- Can stay for up to 2 years as member of English-speaking family
- Help in home for up to five hours per day, 2 days off per week
- You get an allowance and your own room

GENERAL

The scheme is open to single people between 17 and 27 to come to the UK to study English for up to two years as a member of an English-speaking family. You will be required to help in the home for up to five hours a day, and will get at least two full days off a week. In return, you will be paid an allowance and have your own room. The current Home Office recommended allowance is £55 a week.

An au pair must be a national of one of the following countries:

Andorra	Faroe Islands	Romania
Bosnia-Herzegovina	Greenland	San Marino
Republic of Bulgaria	Macedonia	Turkey
Croatia	Monaco	

European Economic Area nationals are not included in the official au pair scheme; but they are free to come to the UK as au pairs.

Nationals of Bosnia-Herzegovina, Bulgaria, Republic of Croatia, Macedonia, Romania, and Turkey must get a visa from their British Embassy or Consulate before they travel to the United Kingdom.

PLAN OF ACTION

To qualify, you must show that: you are not married; you have no dependants; you plan to stay for no more than two years as an au pair; you will not need help from public funds; and you plan to leave the UK when you complete your stay as an au pair. It may be advisable to apply for an entry clearance before travelling to the UK.

Can I move to another 'host' family?

You may move to another 'host' family as long as the new arrangements satisfy the Immigration Rules (see *Chapter 8 – Useful Websites*).

Can I extend my stay as an au pair?

You can apply to extend your stay if you satisfy these conditions: you were given permission to enter the UK as an au pair; you still have an au pair placement; and an extension would not make your stay longer than two years.

If you need general advice about 'au pair' arrangements, one of the organisations listed under that title in the *Appendices* may be able to help.

WRITERS, COMPOSERS, AND ARTISTS

> *AT A GLANCE:*
>
> ◆ For 'creatives' who have built a reputation for original work
> ◆ There are specific criteria which must be met
> ◆ Those who do not meet the criteria will need a work permit
> ◆ Can bring dependants if can support self and family

GENERAL

The main points of this scheme are that you: have built a reputation outside the UK and been involved in producing original published, performed, or exhibited work; intend working only as a self-employed writer, composer, or artist and have supported yourself and any dependants for the last year; continue to support yourself and your dependants from your own income as a writer, composer, or artist without needing any help from public funds.

Check with your Immigration Adviser for a full list of requirements and Home Office definitions of Writers, Authors, Composers, and Artists, as you may need a work permit if you fall into a different category.

You qualify under this section if you are just exhibiting or selling your work, but not staying in the UK.

AIRPORT-BASED OPERATIONAL GROUND STAFF OF OVERSEAS-OWNED AIRLINES

GENERAL

Airport-based operational ground staff of overseas-owned airlines are those who: have been transferred to the UK by an overseas-owned airline (which operates services to and from the UK); work at an international airport as a station manager, security manager, or technical manager; intend to work full-time for the airline; are able to support themselves and any dependants (and live without needing any help from public funds); and do not intend to take employment except as set out above.

Such people may qualify to work without a work permit. See the Home Office website for more information or consult a registered immigration adviser.

TEACHERS AND LANGUAGE ASSISTANTS COMING TO THE UK UNDER APPROVED EXCHANGE SCHEMES

GENERAL

People in this category must: be coming to an educational establishment in the UK under an exchange scheme approved by the Department for Education and Skills (DfES) or run by the British Council's Education and Training Group or the League for the Exchange of Commonwealth Teachers; intend to leave the UK at the end of the exchange period; not intend to take employment except as set out above; and be able to support themselves and any dependants (and live without needing any help from public funds).

The sponsoring organisation (which arranges the exchange) will normally issue teachers with a numbered 'certificate of appointment'. This contains their personal details, and details of where and for how long they will be working. You should show your 'certificate of appointment' to the Entry Clearance Officer when you make your application.

SPECIAL CASES – E.G. TURKEY, BULGARIA...

GENERAL

There are also special schemes for nationals of certain countries, for example Turkey's Ankara Agreement. See the Home Office website for up-to-date information on such Special Cases, or consult a registered immigration adviser.

Chapter 7

H O W 2 Apply for Visas & Entry Clearance

VISAS

> *AT A GLANCE:*
>
> ◆ A certificate put into your passport or travel document overseas
> ◆ Entry Clearance Officers (ECOs) give permission to enter UK
> ◆ UKvisas: government organisation which manages visas in UK Missions
> ◆ UKvisas works closely with Immigration & Nationality Directorate
> ◆ Remember to take all relevant documents in hand luggage
> ◆ Always check the UKvisas website as rules may change

GENERAL

A visa is a certificate that is put into your passport or travel document at a British mission overseas. The visa gives you permission to enter the UK. If you have a valid UK visa, you will not normally be refused entry to the UK unless your circumstances have changed, or you gave false information, or did not tell the Home Office important facts when you applied for your visa.

UKvisas was established jointly by the Foreign and Commonwealth Office and the Home Office to manage the UK's entry clearance (visa) operation.

H O W 2 Apply for Visas & Entry Clearance

Visa or entry clearance applications are processed by entry clearance officers (ECOs) in UK embassies, high commissions, and consulates abroad, collectively known as UK Missions. UKvisas works closely with the Immigration and Nationality Directorate (IND) of the Home Office, the Government department responsible for immigration policy and dealing with applications from people already in the UK to extend their stay; or to change their immigration status.

CATEGORY A, B, AND C VISAS

D FOR ALL OTHER ENTRY CLEARANCES

When you arrive in the UK, an Immigration Officer may ask you questions, so remember to take all relevant documents in your hand luggage. Immigration Officers have the powers to refuse entry.

Entry Clearance is a complex subject, and this chapter is intended as a general guide to procedures. Always check the UKvisas website for full details, or consult your immigration adviser.

ENTRY CLEARANCE – FACTS & FIGURES

> *AT A GLANCE:*
>
> ◆ Process run by UKvisas through British diplomatic posts
> ◆ Over 150 visa sections worldwide, employing over 2000 staff
> ◆ Deals with more than 2 million entry clearance applications per annum

GENERAL

The entry clearance process for the UK is run by UKvisas through British diplomatic posts (UK Missions) around the world.

UKvisas manages over 150 visa sections worldwide, in UK embassies, high commissions, and consulates. The visa operation is largely self-funding through the collection of visa fees.

Over 2,000 staff are directly involved in the overseas visa operation of whom around 100 work in London. Around 900 are UK-based, drawn from the Foreign and Commonwealth and Home Offices, and the remainder locally engaged at overseas posts.

UKvisas handled 2.21 million applications in 2003-04, a rise of nearly 14%.

INFORMATION APPLICABLE TO ALL VISA AND ENTRY CLEARANCE APPLICATIONS

AT A GLANCE:

- May need to apply for entry clearance before you travel
- Depends on nationality and scheme you're applying for
- UKvisas has enquiry form on website
- Visa nationals require visa each time they enter
- Some people will require exit visa clearance from their country
- Visit visas at any relevant office, all other types apply in your country
- Normally need form, passport, photo, visa fee, supporting documents
- You may need an interview with an ECO
- An Immigration Officer will stamp your passport
- If any documents are not genuine, you will be refused entry

GENERAL

If you are currently outside the UK, you may need to apply for entry clearance before you travel. The need to apply for entry clearance will depend on your current nationality and the scheme under which you wish to come to the UK.

UKvisas has a visa enquiry form on its website (see *Chapter 8 – Useful Websites*) which can be used to determine whether you need entry clearance, as well as providing details of the nearest British post where you can make your application. Alternatively, you can consult a qualified registered immigration adviser to find out all the current options.

Non Visa National

If you are not a visa national you do not need a visa to enter the UK as a visitor. You may need to apply for prior entry clearance if you wish to come to the UK for another reason.

Visa Nationals

If you are a national of one of the countries listed in *Appendices (Visa Nationals)* – or if you are stateless, hold a non-national travel document or passport issued by an authority not recognised by the UK – you must hold a valid UK visa on each* occasion that you travel to the UK.

Exit Visas

Some people may need to get an exit visa to leave their country. The visa will include details of the time limit and restrictions as appropriate.

PLAN OF ACTION

The application process depends on the type of visa you require, but in general would be at your nearest British Consulate. You can download the form from the UKvisas website. You can apply for a visit visa at any full service visa-issuing office.

You can apply in a number of ways, for example by post, by courier, in person, and online. The visa section will tell you about the ways in which you can apply.

You will need the following:

1. The relevant application form which you have filled in correctly.

2. Your passport or travel document.

3. The visa fee. This cannot be refunded, and you must normally pay it in the local currency of the country where you are applying.

---

*Visas are not required if you are settled in the UK or if you already have permission to stay in the UK and are returning to the UK before your permission to stay expires.

4. Supporting documents relevant to your application, including all the documents you can to show that you qualify for entry to the UK. If you do not, the Home Office may refuse your application.

5. As a guide, you should include: bank statements, payslips, or some other evidence to show that you can pay for the trip and that you have enough money to support yourself and any dependants without working or getting any help from public funds; and evidence that you intend to leave the UK at the end of your visit (for example, a letter from your employer).

6. If you are visiting family or friends, you will need: a letter from your sponsor (the person you are visiting) explaining your relationship with them and the purpose of your visit. If your sponsor will be supporting you during your visit, or paying for the cost of the visit, you will need: payslips, bank statements, or some other financial evidence to show that they have enough money to support you.

The ECO will try to make a decision using your application form and the supporting documents you have provided. If this is not possible, they will need to interview you.

Upon Arrival in the UK
At the port of entry, the person will need to present all relevant documents and, if appropriate, the visa or entry clearance to an Immigration Officer, who will stamp their passport. For non-visa nationals, details in the passport stamp will indicate the time limit on their stay and restrictions. For visa nationals, the immigration officer will confirm the leave to enter granted by the entry clearance officer.

Important Note – forged or destroyed documents: The Home Office will refuse your application if *any* documents are forged.

Travellers to the UK may commit an offence if they do not produce valid travel documents or passports to the UK immigration authorities for themselves and their children. People found guilty of this offence face up to two years in prison, or a fine (or both).

Check your visa
You should make sure that: your personal details are correct, e.g. purpose, dates etc. If you think that there is anything wrong with your visa, contact the visa section or your immigration adviser immediately.

VISITORS

AT A GLANCE:

- Only visa nationals require entry clearance
- Normal stay is for 6 months

Requirements for a Visitor under the Rules.
The requirements to be met by a person seeking entry clearance as a visitor are that she/he: is genuinely seeking entry as a visitor for a limited period, not exceeding six months; intends to leave the UK at the end of the period of the visit; does not intend to take employment in the UK; does not intend to produce goods or provide services (including the selling of goods or services direct to members of the public) within the United Kingdom; does not intend to study at a maintained school; will maintain and accommodate him/herself and any dependants adequately; and can meet the cost of the return or onward journey.

Only visa nationals require entry clearance to enter the UK as a visitor. Other nationals may wish to apply for entry clearance where they are in doubt about their admissibility, and they are encouraged to do so.

WORK PERMIT HOLDERS

> *AT A GLANCE:*
>
> ◆ Non-EEA nationals need entry clearance if for more than 6 months
> ◆ Stay less than 6 months: entry clearance not required, but recommended
> ◆ Clearance will be given for full period of work permit stay
> ◆ Visa and work permit criteria are separate, so entry not guaranteed
> ◆ Dependants can generally come too, but with certain exceptions

Work permit holders who are non-EEA nationals (including non-visa nationals) who wish to come to the UK for more than 6 months must obtain entry clearance before travelling. This does not apply to new EU member states.

Entry clearance will normally be granted for the full period of the work permit.

Dependants

The spouse, unmarried partner, and children of a work permit holder may apply for entry clearance as the dependants of a work permit holder. They will be given conditions of stay which do not place any restrictions, other than those that would apply to a resident worker, on their taking employment or engaging in business. In other words, your dependants will be allowed to work in any occupational category.

The exceptions to this are the dependants of Multiple Entry, Student Internships, and Sectors Based Scheme work permit holders who, if they wish to accompany a work permit holder to the UK, must qualify for entry in their own right under another category of the Immigration Rules.

The criteria for issuing a visa or entry clearance are separate from those of work permits. The granting of a work permit does not guarantee that a visa or entry clearance will be issued. In addition, the granting of a work permit does not guarantee entry to the UK.

DOMESTIC WORKERS

> *AT A GLANCE:*
>
> - Complete form *VAF1 – non-settlement*
> - Supporting documents include job confirmation, including terms

Supporting documents
You should include all the documents you can to show that you qualify for entry to the UK as an overseas domestic worker. As a guide, you should include: written confirmation from your employer that they will support you and give you somewhere to live; and a written copy of your main terms and conditions of employment.

BUSINESS OR EMPLOYMENT-RELATED VISITS

> *AT A GLANCE:*
>
> - Includes those visiting for interviews, auditions, or 'trials'
> - Difference from Business Person is that business remains outside UK
> - Visits are for 6 months

GENERAL
The Rules differentiate between a business visitor and a person setting up or engaging in business in the UK who is required to qualify under separate provisions. Business visitors must qualify under the requirements of the Rules for visitors.

The Home Office will need to be satisfied that the applicant: intends to transact business directly linked to his or her employment abroad; normally lives and works abroad and has no intention of transferring the base to the UK, even temporarily;

receives a salary from abroad (but may get reasonable expenses to cover travel and subsistence during the visit).

There is an extensive list of Business visitor's definitions on the UKvisas website. Examples include: attending meetings, conferences, trade fairs, seminars, delivering goods from abroad, negotiating or signing trade agreements and contracts, attending interviews, including sportspeople going for 'trials', entertainers going for auditions, and those coming to undertake fact-finding missions. Can also include: journalists on a short assignment, advisers, consultants, trainers, and trouble shooters, provided that they are employed abroad.

The following should not be treated as business visitors: employees of overseas firms whose involvement with a UK subsidiary amounts to employment here; consultants who are self-employed, other than those contracted abroad by an overseas firm with a UK subsidiary; those who are undertaking productive work which could be undertaken by someone recruited from the local or EEA labour force; those offering training, unless such training involves products manufactured overseas, or is specific to the operation of a group of companies of which the UK firm is a member.

Job interviews, auditions or 'trials'

People wishing to come to the UK to attend job interviews are treated as business visitors. Entry Clearance Officer's (ECOs) will need to be satisfied that prior arrangement for interview has been made. In the case of candidates for enlistment in the UK armed forces, the Ministry of Defence will provide suitable candidates with a letter for presentation to an ECO when entry clearance is required. Similarly, entertainers or sports persons who wish to come for auditions or trials (e.g. footballers) are travelling for the purpose of 'job interviews' and are deemed to be business visitors.

Internationally famous people wishing to appear on radio or

television for an interview, as opposed to performing, (possibly earning a fee in the process) should also be treated as business visitors.

As long as the persons described in this section are travelling on a one-off basis and only intend staying in the UK for a short visit, ECOs are likely to treat their applications as in the business visitors category. If any of these persons intend to further their careers in the UK by engaging in their profession here, e.g. a footballer playing in a match, a singer participating in a concert, an actor starring in a film etc, the application should be dealt with as for employment.

WORKING HOLIDAYMAKERS

AT A GLANCE:

- ◆ For Commonwealth citizens aged between 17 and 30
- ◆ You need a visa, which starts from date of entry and lasts 2 years
- ◆ May need to show your available funds
- ◆ May need to show evidence of travel plans

GENERAL
You may stay in the UK as a working holidaymaker for two years from the date you enter. You should tell the Entry Clearance Officer when you plan to travel so that your visa can start from that date. The visa can start any time up to three months from the date of issue.

PLAN OF ACTION
As well as visa application form and related requirements, you may also need to show: evidence of how much money you have;

and evidence of any travel plans you have made, such as a provisional travel booking.

The Entry Clearance Officer will check that they have all the information they need to make a decision. If they need more information, they may ask you to come back with additional documents before they can accept your application. Once they have accepted your application, they may need to interview you.

VISITORS GETTING MARRIED BUT NOT SETTLING

> *AT A GLANCE:*
>
> ◆ Treated as a visit if couple intend to leave UK after marriage
> ◆ Those subject to immigration control need entry clearance
> ◆ May get a multiple entry visa in some circumstances
> ◆ Must prove coming to give notice or get married
> ◆ Different rules for Scotland

GENERAL

In cases where a person wishes to visit the UK to get married, after which the couple will leave to live elsewhere, the application will be treated as a visit. If either you – or your future husband or wife – are not EEA (European Economic Area) or Swiss nationals, you can visit the UK together to get married, as long as you intend to leave the country within six months.

PLAN OF ACTION

Everyone coming to the UK to get married (except EEA and Swiss nationals) must get a 'visit for marriage' entry clearance or visa, unless you will marry in an Anglican Church (visa nationals must still get a visit visa).

For those applying to marry in Scotland, where it is possible to give notice of marriage by post, the visit visa must be a valid one. Post-dated visas, which do not become valid until after notice of marriage is given, will not be accepted by registrars. Unless specially requested, visas will be valid from the date of their issue.

For those already in the UK, a Certificate of Approval must be obtained from the Home Office instead. Certificates will only be issued to those with more than six months valid leave to enter and who have three months or more leave remaining. This means that persons who hold a visit visa, illegal entrants, over-stayers, and failed asylum seekers will not usually be able to get married in the United Kingdom. Holders of entry clearance will not be required to apply for the certificate of approval, as the entry clearance will act in lieu of the certificate.

ACADEMIC VISITORS

GENERAL
During a vacation or a 'sabbatical' year, or between jobs, academics may make arrangements to join others working in the same field to take part in their research work or to do a little teaching (or both).

They will usually obtain such posts through contacts with other academics or direct arrangements between university faculties, not through formal job advertisements (e.g. for academic workers). The primary reason for taking on the work should be to widen their knowledge, experience, and contacts.

Although there is no specific provision for the entry of such persons (they cannot be regarded as students), those who fulfil the following conditions may be allowed entry into the UK as academic visitors under a concession outside the Rules.

Those who may qualify include: post-graduate researchers – not students – (if sponsored by the Royal Society, the British Council, a charitable educational, or research organisation, a national research council, e.g. the Medical Research Council, or an institution of further or higher education, e.g. a university); academics taking part in formal exchange arrangements with UK counterparts (including doctors); senior doctors/dentists taking part in research, teaching or clinical practice; academics from an overseas institution who wish to use sabbatical leave to carry out research; visiting lecturers going for a single lecture or a lecture series.

PLAN OF ACTION

Academic visitors must fulfil the following criteria: they will not receive funds from a UK source (except payments of scholarships, grants, bursaries, expenses, reasonable honoraria, and payments on exchange basis); and they do not intend filling a genuine, substantive, vacancy; and the stay is incidental to, or in preparation for, a career abroad; and the stay will not exceed 12 months.

Some examples of those who do not qualify are: research students undertaking PhD or other postgraduate studies at a UK academic institution who are studying under supervision for a recognised higher qualification (usually a Masters degree or a Doctorate), or are seeking to further studies/research in some other acceptable form – they are regarded as students under the Rules; academic workers are normally in paid posts which are advertised – they may well be working alongside postgraduate students – these people are considered to be in employment and require work permits.

Spouse and dependants
Academic visitors are entitled to have their spouse and dependants accompany or join them in UK, provided the spouse and dependants do not intend to take employment in UK, and that they can be supported without recourse to Public Funds. Applicants will be treated in the same way as a spouse or dependant of a student. Dependants are granted Leave to Enter in line with the principle applicant.

MEDICAL TREATMENT VISITORS

GENERAL
You can apply for a visit visa to travel to the UK for private medical treatment. You must be able to show that you: have made suitable arrangements for the necessary consultation or treatment; have enough money to pay for the treatment; have enough money to support yourself and live without working or getting any help from public funds while you are in the UK; and intend to leave the UK at the end of your treatment.

You may also be asked to provide the following: a doctor's letter giving details of your medical condition and the treatment you need; confirmation that you have made suitable arrangements for the consultation or treatment and how long the treatment will last; evidence that you can afford to pay for the consultation and treatment.

You may also be asked to give an undertaking (in other words, a formal agreement) that you will pay for the consultation and treatment.

FOREIGN ARMED FORCES PERSONNEL VISITORS

GENERAL

Foreign armed forces personnel who come to the UK for training or familiarisation courses with British firms are not exempt from control. Visa nationals will therefore require entry clearance and this may be granted subject to confirmation that proper arrangements have been made.

Servicemen travelling to the UK under this category should be advised to carry confirmation of the duration of their courses or official duties with them so that this can be shown to the Immigration Officer if necessary.

Members of foreign armed forces personnel travelling to attend training or familiarisation courses will be issued with entry clearances endorsed '*D: COURSE F*'.

VISITORS IN TRANSIT

GENERAL

If you are a visa national, you will need a visa to enter the UK even if you are passing through the UK on your way to another country (known as 'in transit'). Use the 'Do I need a UK visa?' questionnaire on the UKvisas website to find out more.

If you will be staying in the UK for less than 48 hours before you continue your journey, you will need to obtain a 'visitor in transit' visa. If you want to stay in the UK for longer than 48 hours, you will need to apply for a visit visa.

An Immigration Officer may decide to let you travel through the UK without holding a 'visitor in transit' visa. This is known as the 'transit without visa concession' (TWOV).

If you are a visa national transiting the UK by sea and land on your way to Ireland, the Channel Islands, or the Isle of Man, you will need a visit visa for the UK.

If you are a visa national transiting the UK by sea and land on your way from Ireland, the Channel Islands, or the Isle of Man to another country, you will need a visitor in transit, or a visit visa for the UK.

If you are passing through the UK by air, you may qualify for the 'transit without visa' (TWOV) concession.

TWOV Concession
To qualify you must: arrive on a cruise ship and leave on the same ship within 24 hours; arrive and leave by air within 24 hours, and have no intention of staying in the UK (you can travel by rail or road between two airports); or hold a confirmed booking on a flight or ship that will leave within 24 hours of your arrival in the UK.

You must also: have the documents you need to enter the country you are travelling to; and have the documents you need for any other country that you may pass through on your journey.

Nationalities Excluded from the TWOV Concession
This concession does not apply to certain visa nationals who must have a visa to pass through the UK on their way to another country, even if they are not entering the UK or changing airports. This is known as a 'direct airside transit' visa (DATV). If you are a national of one of the countries listed under 'Visa Nationals' (see *Appendices*), you will need to have a valid UK DATV.

If you have a DATV, you will not be able to pass through UK immigration control. You will not usually be allowed to stay in the UK overnight to wait for a connection to continue your journey.

If you are a direct airside transit (DAT) national and passing through the UK on your way to or from the Republic of Ireland, the Channel Islands, or the Isle of Man, you need a visit visa for the UK, unless you are exempt from the DAT requirement.

SETTLING IN THE UK

Applying

Apart from the visa forms, you should include all the documents you can to show that you qualify for entry to the UK as a husband, wife, or partner.

As a guide, you should include: your birth certificate; your marriage certificate (if you are married); your sponsor's birth certificate; recent statements or letters from your sponsor's UK employer, bank, local authority, or building society to show what support and accommodation will be available for you in the UK; letters from you and your sponsor that are relevant to your application; a divorce certificate or death certificate of your husband's or wife's previous wife or husband (if either of you have been married before); and evidence that your sponsor is settled in the UK – this can be a copy of their passport or registration certificate that has been confirmed as a true copy, in other words, certified. (See also *Chapter 4*.)

Please check your child's visa when you get it. You should make sure that: the child's personal details are correct; it correctly states the purpose for which the child wants to come to the UK; and it is valid for the date on which the child will travel. (You can ask for it to be post-dated for up to three months if the child will not be travelling immediately.)

Applying for entry clearance can be complex, and you may wish to consult a registered Immigration Adviser.

Chapter 8

H O W 2 Get Started

ACTION PLAN

> *AT A GLANCE:*
>
> ◆ Believe in yourself
> ◆ Write down your goals, purpose, and objectives
> ◆ Evaluate your skills and qualifications
> ◆ Research the market, gather information
> ◆ Review your options, decide your priorities
> ◆ Write an ACTION PLAN
> ◆ Take ACTION… or nothing will happen!

A person without a goal is like a ship without a rudder

GENERAL

You must have a written list of goals, a definite date for the attainment of those goals, and an Action Plan. You must believe in yourself, have confidence in your ability and the persistence to see your plan through. There are many books available on setting and achieving goals. Amazon.com lists 65 books under the category of 'setting goals', from bestselling authors such as Brian Tracy, Zig Ziglar, and Jim Rohn, and we would urge you to read them. However, a simple way to get you started today is to write down the following three questions:

i. Where am I now?
ii. Where do I want to be?
iii. What steps do I have to take to get there?

Where am I now?
Be realistic. What skills and qualifications do you possess and, more importantly, what value can you give to the marketplace? Let's say your goal is to come to the UK to work. Is your current occupation in demand or on the official Home Office 'shortage occupations' list? (see *Chapter 1*) Are there job vacancies listed in your field? (see below, *Useful Websites*) Are your skills in demand and, if not, can you study to gain those skills? Think of yourself as a business or a corporation, and think of your skills or labour as your 'product' to *sell* to the marketplace.

Now ask yourself this question: Is there a market for my 'product'? If there is, great, you're in business! If, however, after doing your research you find that there is no market for your product, decide what you are going to do about it. Write it all down now!

Where do I want to be?
What are your goals, objectives, and purpose in life? What course of study do you wish to take? What job would you like, or what type of business would you like to start? Which places would you like to visit? Where would you like to be in 3, 5, or 10 years from now? What country would you like to be living in? What sort of house would you like to own? What car would you like to be driving? What lifestyle do you aspire to? Write it all down now!

What steps do I have to take to get there?
What do you have to *do* to achieve your goal? What will you have to *give* in return for a better life? There is no such thing as something for nothing, and there is always a price to pay if you

want to be successful or achieve a goal. Only you can decide whether or not the price you will have to pay to reach your goal is worth it.

What information do you need to gather to achieve your objectives? The internet is the ideal place to start your research, and many useful sites are listed in this chapter. We have never had so much information literally at our fingertips! If you don't own a computer, borrow one, use a college, library, or internet café. If you don't know how to use a computer, find someone who does and get them to help you or, better still, take a course in Information Technology (IT). You are seriously handicapped in today's world without IT skills.

Review your options, and decide on your priorities. Decide what daily, weekly, and monthly action you need to take to move you closer to your goal. Whatever your situation, start taking ACTION! Right now, take a clean sheet of paper and write out a simple PLAN. Even if your plan is a simple list of goals and objectives, the important thing is to GET STARTED and to write it all down now!

GETTING STARTED ON YOUR ACTION PLAN

GENERAL
The first step of your plan to come to the UK will be to decide whether you want to Work, Study, Visit, or Settle. We have provided the table on the following two pages to help you evaluate your options.

H O W 2 Get Started

WHAT IS THE PURPOSE OF YOUR TRIP TO THE UK?

WORK	BUSINESS	STUDY	SETTLE	VISIT	OTHER SCHEMES
Work permit	Business person	Overseas student	Spouse	Tourist visitor	Permit-free employment
Sectors Based Scheme	Sole representative	Student nurse	Fiancé(e)		Entertainer
Student internship	Investor	Writing up thesis	Unmarried partner	Academic visitor	Sportspeople
Highly Skilled Migrant Programme	Innovator	Re-sit examination	Same sex partner	Business visitor	Writer, composer, artist
	EC Association Agreement	Students' Union sabbatical officer	Children	Medical Treatment visitor	Representative of overseas media organisation
Ancestry		Postgraduate dentist	Adopted children	Student visitor	Access Rights to resident child
Workers Registration Scheme – new EU members		Postgraduate doctor	Dependant relatives	Visitor in transit	Teacher and language assistant
Offshore worker		EEA student	Parents and grandparents	Carer	Au Pair
Short-term worker		Overseas doctor coming for PLAB tests	Residency	Marriage or fiancé(e)	Minister of religion
Representative of overseas insurance company			Citizenship	Relative acting as childminder	Film crew on location
Jewish Agency				Job interview	Overseas government employee
Working holidaymaker				Minister of religion	Science and engineering graduate
				Archaeological dig visitor	Japan Youth Exchange Scheme
				Amateur entertainer	Gap year entrants for work in schools

H O W 2 Come to the UK

WORK	BUSINESS	STUDY	SETTLE	VISIT	OTHER SCHEMES
				Amateur sportsperson	Voluntary Overseas Worker
				Appeal hearing	Fresh Talent Working in Scotland scheme
					Citizen of Switzerland, EEA and UK
					Operational ground staff of overseas airline
					Special Cases… e.g. Turkey, Bulgaria
					Domestic worker or Private servant of a diplomat

Perhaps this is your goal!

WORKING OR STUDYING IN THE UK – GETTING STARTED

If your plan is to work or study, it may be useful to find out how your qualifications compare with the UK equivalent, and have your English language skills assessed by an internationally recognised organisation.

NARIC – National Recognition Information Centre

AT A GLANCE:

- People applying for jobs or study courses are often asked for a NARIC
- You may also require an IELTS English Language test
- Education UK and UCAS websites are a place for students to start
- The UK Government Job Centre website is a place to look for jobs
- The 'Work Permits (UK)' website is a good general site for workers

GENERAL

UK NARIC is the national agency under contract to the UK Government Department for Education and Skills. It is the official source of information and advice on the comparability of international qualifications – from over 180 countries worldwide – with those in the UK.

NARIC provides information on the comparability of international and national qualifications in regard to education and training, professional registration, and international employment. The information from NARIC about education systems and technical or vocational qualifications is recognised by higher education institutions, professional bodies, and commercial organisations.

NARIC Assessment

Although not a compulsory requirement, overseas applicants applying for UK jobs, work permits, or student places are often asked for a NARIC Assessment to compare their overseas qualifications with the UK equivalent.

If you have a credit card, you can apply online through NARIC (see *Useful Websites*). Alternatively, if you do not wish to use a credit card, or if you require help and advice about NARIC, Overseas Consultancy Services can apply on your behalf. Download the NARIC Request forms from Overseas Consultancy Services website www.overseasconsultancy.com.

IELTS

The **International English Language Testing System (IELTS)** is an internationally owned and globally recognised direct English language assessment of the highest quality and integrity, readily available throughout the world.

IELTS is jointly managed by the University of Cambridge Local Examination Syndicate, the British Council, and IDP Education Australia. It is designed to assess the language ability of candidates who need to study or work where English is used as a language of communication. For more information, check out the IELTS website (www.ielts.org).

What if I clearly speak English but have not taken the IELTS test?

For persons with existing English skills, for example, those educated in an English speaking nation, Entry Clearance Officers may apply discretion to allow entry where evidence is provided that an individual speaks competent English.

STUDENTS – THE FIRST STEPS

The world-class academic and social reputation of the UK means more and more students are choosing to study here.

According to figures published by the Universities and Colleges Admissions Service (UCAS) in the UK, the number of students from outside the European Union (EU) taking up places at UK universities and colleges has increased by 9%.

China is now the third largest supplier of overseas students to the UK. Enrolments from students in countries in Africa, such as Ghana, Zimbabwe, and Nigeria, also increased significantly in recent years.

Recent figures from UCAS show that nearly 11 per cent of the accepted applicants to higher education in the UK are now from overseas; the majority are postgraduates. There are more than 300,000 international students from more than 180 countries in the UK currently, and the British Council believes this could rise to more than 800,000 by the year 2018.

Mark Bickerton, Director of the International Office at the University of North London in the UK, has seen increasing numbers of international student applications and enrolments at his institution. He says: 'I would say that the biggest impact [on international enrolments] has been the availability of the Internet and email.'

Getting Started

The UK's education brand has been given a boost with the development of an Education UK website by the British Council (see *Useful Websites*). The site offers a comprehensive, fully searchable listing of courses available for international students in the UK, along with information on visas, fees, accommodation, the UK education system, applications through UCAS, and living in the UK.

Some UK universities recruit huge numbers of overseas

students – more than half the students at the London School of Economics are from overseas, for example, and other universities, including world-famous ones, are keen to recruit more. Oxford University plans to gradually increase the numbers of overseas students it accepts.

Universities have international offices on campus to support foreign students, and some universities have offices throughout the world – Middlesex University near London has 14 around the globe.

Course Options

There is a huge range of choice in regard to courses. A lot of overseas students in the UK choose vocational (occupational) degree courses. These can form the first part of the training necessary to enter certain professions – like accountancy, engineering, and international law, which can exempt you from some professional exams – although make sure that they are accepted in your country. Take a look online at the UCAS website (see *Useful Websites*) at the range of courses on offer, and you may well be astonished.

The UCAS application system is also very straightforward. It allows you to apply to up to six universities or higher education colleges for one low fee, and everything is then handled centrally – a boon to students in far flung parts of the world.

Financial Help

You might be able to get financial support to study here because some universities give bursaries to overseas students who would otherwise not be able to afford to come. One of these is Westminster University in London, which gives bursaries worth £1.2m a year, many of them to overseas students.

Awards range from £1,000 reduction in fees to a package worth up to £20,000 including visa and flights. Before awarding a bursary, the university will look for academic excellence, financial need, and confidence that the student will return to their country and contribute there.

English Language Assistance
There is a huge advantage to be gained by studying in the original home of a language which is spoken throughout the world. If your English could be a bit better, you will be able to take advantage of English language classes which many UK universities provide free of charge to overseas students.

Will I feel left out as a foreign student?
UK higher education institutions have a long tradition of caring for their international students. For example, you may well be collected from the airport or your port of entry, and transported to your university or college. Once there, you are likely to be given a welcome party and an orientation tour of the area. You will also have a personal tutor to turn to, plus support staff in the international office should you need any kind of help.

Universities and colleges with international students generally have an international society so that you can meet people from your own and other countries. Societies such as these are likely to put on social events and trips out to some of the most beautiful parts of the UK.

The range of societies and clubs that you will find at a typical UK university is extraordinary, covering all kinds of interests from mainstream sport to some more obscure interests.

Cutting Edge Teaching Facilities
The UK higher education system offers cutting-edge and world-leading research opportunities, internationally recognised degrees, and relevant high-quality, high-standard training.

Culture and Religion
All the major religions are catered for, and prayer/worship

facilities will be available to you. The multicultural nature of many of Britain's towns and cities will ensure that you should be able to buy a plentiful supply of the ingredients you need for a taste of home cooking.

Medical Care
One other major bonus of your stay will normally qualify for free healthcare under the National Health Service if your course lasts longer than six months.

The government is fully supporting the drive towards many more overseas students coming to the UK to study. The British Council said, 'As part of the Prime Minister's initiative, we are looking to build a site that will transform the process of finding out about and applying for educational courses in the UK.'

Whatever your reason for choosing the UK for your education, you have chosen wisely and can expect a warm welcome. So GET STARTED and APPLY NOW.

WORKERS – THE FIRST STEPS

AT A GLANCE:

- Asses your skills
- Search for jobs, send CV and apply
- Secure an employer
- Employer obtains work permit
- Apply for entry clearance
- Book flights!

GENERAL
The UK Job Market The working population in the UK is just under 30 million people. Job Centre Plus (see Useful Websites below), the government agency, reports that key employment

sectors such as wholesale and retail trade; manufacturing; health and social work; and real estate, renting, and business activities – including IT and professional services – together account for over half of the UK workforce.

The adult rate of the minimum wage – for workers aged 22 and over – is £4.85 per hour at time of going to press (June 2005). This will increase to £5.05 per hour in October 2005, and to £5.35 in October 2006.

There is no maximum salary or wage. Philip Green, one of Britain's richest men, earned a staggering £201 million in dividends from his BHS business last year.

Some of the largest employers include companies like Tesco Stores, Sainsbury's Supermarkets, ASDA, GlaxoSmithKline, British American Tobacco, Royal Mail, and a number of banks such as The Royal Bank of Scotland, Lloyds TSB, HSBC, and Barclays. The government is a major employer in areas such as the National Health Service (NHS), Civil Service, and Post Office.

Over the past five years, the workforce in the UK has expanded at an average rate of 0.8% annually. Employment growth has been driven largely by significant increases in the numbers working within public administration and defence; education; construction; health and social work; and real estate, renting, and business activities.

Certain jobs are classified as 'hard-to-fill' vacancies which include: working in hotels and restaurants; education; and health and social work. Construction, manufacturing, and transport, and distribution employers in Wales also report problems recruiting.

A higher ratio of vacancies occurs in certain areas of the country, in particular the North West, Yorkshire, and Humber, the West Midlands, and the South East. In Northern Ireland, elementary occupations and technical and associate professional occupations appear to prove the hardest to fill, with approximately one in five employers reporting hard to fill vacancies for such roles.

TREND INDICATORS

Unmet labour demand: dentists; nursing and midwifery professionals; doorkeepers; watchpersons and related workers; meat- and fish-processing machine operators; bus and tram drivers; heavy truck and lorry drivers; helpers and cleaners in offices, hotels, and other establishments; cooks; institution-based personal care workers; shop sales persons and demonstrators; social work associate professionals; receptionists and information clerks; primary education teaching associate professionals.

Unmet job demand: mining and quarrying labourers; construction and maintenance labourers for roads, dams, and similar projects; assembling labourers; freight handlers; car, taxi and van drivers; machine-tool operators.

FIVE SOURCES TO HELP YOU FIND A JOB

The jobs are out there if you know where to look. These are just five resources which will lead you to boundless opportunities:

1. The Internet. One of the best sources for job hunting is the internet (see *Useful Websites* below). For example, Jobcentre Plus, the government employment service, currently lists over 700,000 job vacancies on its website. The employment agency, Reed, lists around 240,000 jobs on its site. That's almost 1 million jobs on just two sites! You can also use the internet to apply direct to large employers like the NHS (*see Useful Websites*).

2. Newspapers and Job Magazines. There are huge on-line resources and listings for jobs and business opportunities published by newspapers and magazines on their websites. For instance, *The Times on-line* currently lists hundreds of jobs on its website. There is also a very useful section on 'How to Find Jobs' covering everything from Accountancy to Youth Prison

Officer. Most national UK Newspapers and Specialist Magazines, such as the *Nursing Times,* now have excellent on-line job sites (see *Useful Sites* below) covering a myriad of jobs in every sector.

3. Specialist agencies. There are also specialist employment agencies helping people to find work abroad, although you should only use reputable agencies approved by the authorities in your country.

4. Multinational companies. Large international companies are an obvious source of both locally based and overseas jobs. Many multinationals transfer staff abroad on Intra Company Work Permits (*see Chapter 1*).

5. Relatives and friends. Relatives, friends, and contacts already in the UK can provide a valuable source of available jobs and will often make the introduction for you.

SEVEN TIPS ON WRITING & PRESENTING YOUR CV

There are whole books written on this subject; however, here are 7 basic rules you should follow:

1. The 'golden' rule is K.I.S.S. – KEEP IT SHORT AND SIMPLE! Employers will not want to read long, boring CVs; a few pages will usually be sufficient.

2. List your employment history first, starting with the most recent job.

3. Always check your English grammar and spelling. Employers will be put off by a poorly written CV or letter. Microsoft Word has excellent tools to check spelling and grammar, but do not rely on this alone. Get someone to proof read it for you.

4. Include a brief description of your duties.

5. Write a short covering letter and address it to a named person rather than 'to whom it may concern' or 'the manager'.

6. Include a smiling picture.

7. If in doubt, hire a professional to write your CV.

When you have done all that, get posting and emailing!

The Right Skills
You need to assess your skills and qualifications (see NARIC) to see if they fit both the job and work permit criteria. Be honest with yourself… do you need further training or study?

Obtaining a Work Permit
Employers will arrange your work permit or appoint an immigration specialist to apply on their behalf and make all the arrangements. In order to obtain a work permit (other than HSMP), both the employee and employer must meet the requirements in order to qualify. This is where a specialist immigration adviser can often help.

Immigration Advisers will be able to arrange a work permit provided you have a suitable job. Advisers and agencies arranging work permits in the UK must be registered with the Office of the Immigration Services Commissioner (OISC).

Agencies will often arrange the work permit on behalf of the employer if they are supplying staff.

Work Permits issued under the HSMP are applied for by the individual, as you do not need an employer when you apply. For more information on Work Permits and Business categories see *Chapter 1*.

VISITING THE UK – THE FIRST STEPS

> *AT A GLANCE:*
>
> ◆ Visit must not be for more than six months
> ◆ Must intend to leave at end of visit
> ◆ You need enough money to live without working or public funds
> ◆ Visa required from certain countries

GENERAL

Having decided that you want to come to the UK as a visitor, there are a number of things you should bear in mind before applying for a visa. You need to consider the purpose of your visit and whether or not another type of visa may be more appropriate.

Whether you are visiting the UK for business or social reasons, you can only stay for a maximum of six months. If you often visit the UK, you can apply for a visa that is valid for one, two, five, or ten years. You can then visit the UK as often as you like while your visa is still valid, but you can only stay for up to six months on each visit.

Different types of visitors will need different paperwork. Check what type of visa you need. (See *Chapter 6* for requirements that relate to your visitor status, and *Appendices* for relevant lists). Make sure you have all the Entry Requirements before you travel, and make sure you bring them with you!

Make sure you check your visa when you get it, especially personal details and purpose of visit and dates. If you think there is anything wrong with your visa, contact the visa section immediately.

Can I study in the UK? As a visitor, you can study during your stay. You can only apply to stay longer than six months if you are accepted on a course of study at degree level or above, or you entered the UK with a student or prospective student visa.

You can get more information from the guidance on the *UKvisas* website (see *Useful Websites* below). We recommend you use the 'Do I need a UK visa?' questionnaire on that website. See also *Chapters 3* and *7*.

SETTLING IN THE UK – THE FIRST STEPS

> *AT A GLANCE:*
>
> ◆ You can qualify on own status or that of a relative / dependant
> ◆ First apply for indefinite leave to remain / permanent residence
> ◆ The requirements vary depending on your status
> ◆ You can then apply for naturalisation / British citizenship
> ◆ The rules are different for spouses of British citizens

GENERAL
You can qualify either through your own status, through, for example, a scheme such as HSMP, or you will qualify because you are a relative and/or dependant of someone else who qualifies to settle.

Indefinite leave to remain / permanent residence
A non-EEA national may apply for indefinite leave to remain or permanent residency within the UK. Depending on the status of yourself or your relative/dependant, you will have to wait between two and ten years before you can apply. The first step is to check if and when you qualify, and then make your application, ensuring that you include all the relevant requirements, such as employer's letter and passport copies.

After indefinite leave to remain (permanent residence) has

been granted, you may remain in the UK permanently and take up any kind of work.

Naturalisation / British Citizenship

Once you have gained settled ('permanent residency') status you can apply to be 'naturalised' as a British citizen. Again, the first step is to check if and when you qualify, and then make your application, ensuring that you include all the relevant requirements, such as employer's letter and passport copies. Note that there are different rules for people who are married to a British citizen.

See *Chapter 4* for more on Settlement in the UK.

USEFUL CONTACTS

UK GOVERNMENT ADVICE WHEN ABROAD OR IN UK

Advice for people who are abroad
People abroad can get advice from a Government representative overseas at the British Embassy, Consulate, or High Commission in the country where they reside.

UKvisas
For information on visa and entry clearance requirements, either contact a British Embassy, Consulate, or High Commission overseas, or contact:
UKvisas, London SW1A 2AH
General enquiries: (+44) (0)20 7008 8438
Application forms: (+44) (0)20 7008 8308
Email: www.ukvisas.gov.uk/enquiries

Leaflets on immigration matters
You can download leaflets on immigration matters from the internet or by phoning the Home Office Information Leaflets line on 0870 241 0645 or UKvisas' Public Enquiry line on 020 7008 8438.

H O W 2 Come to the UK

Home Office Worker Registration Team
Work Permits (UK), PO BOX 3468, Sheffield, S3 8WA
Tel: 0114 259 6262
Email: WPcustomers@ind.homeoffice.gsi.gov.uk
Website: www.workingintheuk.gov.uk

Immigration and Nationality Enquiries Bureau (INEB)
Tel: 0870 606 7766

Immigration and Nationality Directorate (IND)
Croydon Public Caller Unit, Lunar House; 40 Wellesley Road, Croydon CR9 2BY.
General enquiries: (+44) (0)870 606 7766
Application forms: (+44) (0)870 241 0645
Email: indpublicenquiries@ind.homeoffice.gsi.gov.uk
Website: www.ind.homeoffice.gov.uk

Immigration Advisory Service (IAS)
The IAS is an independent charity that gives confidential advice and help, and can represent people who are applying for a visa for the UK. Contact:
IAS, 3rd Floor, County House, 190 Great Dover Street, London SE1 4YB.
Telephone: (+44) (0)20 7967 1200
Duty office (open 24 hours a day) - (+44) (0)20 8814 1559
Fax: (+44) (0)20 7403 5875
Email: advice@iasuk.org
Website: www.iasuk.org

Student Visas
Students seeking a Register of establishments for which they can get a Student Visa should see the register on the DfES website:
www.dfes.gov.uk/providersregister

Embassies
The address and telephone number of your embassy should be listed in the London telephone book, or you can telephone directory enquiries on 118 500.

Marriage and Register Offices
For more information about marriage and register offices, contact the relevant General Register Office:
England and Wales - www.gro.gov.uk
Scotland - www.gro-scotland.gov.uk
Northern Ireland - www.groni.gov.uk

H O W 2 Get Started

STUDENTS & EDUCATION

British Council
For the creation of partnerships between UK and other cultures, contact:
www.britcoun.org

Education UK
Website for overseas students, run by the British Council.
www.educationuk.org

Universities and Colleges Admission System (UCAS)
www.ucas.com

International English Language Testing System (IELTS)
For testing your English skills: www.ielts.org

The Association of Recognised English Language Services (ARELS)
This is the association of all private English language schools, which is officially recognised by The British Council.

British Association of State English Language Teaching (BASELT)
This is the association of all universities and colleges offering English language courses, which is officially recognised by The British Council.

National Recognition Information Centre (NARIC)
UK NARIC is the national agency under contract to the UK Government Department for Education and Skills. It is the official source of information and advice on the comparability of international qualifications – from over 180 countries worldwide – with those in the UK.
UK NARIC, Oriel House, Oriel Road, Cheltenham, Glos GL50 1XP.
Tel: +44 (0)870 9904088; Fax: +44 (0)870 990 1560
Email: info@naric.org.uk

Learn Direct
Learn Direct is an organisation that can provide free advice on English language learning in your area. There may be a charge for the courses that are available.
Helpline: 0800 100900.

FINDING A JOB

Jobcentre Plus website: www.jobcentreplus.gov.uk
The Jobcentre Plus website contains thousand of job vacancies in the UK.

EURES
The European Job Mobility Portal: a way to find information on jobs and learning opportunities in Europe.
http://europa.eu.int/eures/index.jsp

WORKER ENQUIRIES, INFORMATION & REPRESENTATION

Department of Health
www.doh.gov.uk

Department for Work and Pensions
Tel: 0207 712 2171
www.dwp.gov.uk

National Insurance number
To get a National Insurance number, you must make an appointment for an 'evidence of identity' interview at the nearest Job Centre. This is a government office which can be found in most large towns or city districts. You will need to take proof of identity (such as a passport) as well as evidence that you are working. You can find the nearest office in the telephone directory, or visit www.dwp.gov.uk/lifeevent/benefits/ni_number.asp.

Health & Safety Executive
HSE Infoline, Caerphilly Business Park, Caerphilly CF83 3GG.
Tel: 08701 545500
Minicom: 02920 808537
Email: hseinfomationservices@natbrit.com
Website: www.hse.gov.uk

National Minimum Wage Helpline
Tel 0845 6000 678

Agricultural Wages Board Helplines
England or Wales: 0845 000 134
Scotland: 0131 244 6392
Northern Ireland: 02890 520813 or 02890 524492

BUSINESS, COMPANIES & COMMERCIAL

Newly Self-employed Helpline
Tel 08459 154515

H O W 2 Get Started

Trade Partners UK
For advice and information from the Government to help UK companies trade internationally, contact: www.tradepartners.gov.uk

Department of Trade and Industry (DTI)
For general information on the world of work: www.dti.gov.uk

Companies House
For registration and provision of company information, contact:
www.companies-house.gov.uk

British Chambers of Commerce
For business information and advice, contact: www.chamberonline.co.uk

Small Business Service (SBS)
For general business advice, contact: www.sbs.gov.uk

REPRESENTATIVE BODIES

General Medical Council (GMC)
For more information about registering as a doctor in the United Kingdom, please write to:
The General Medical Council, Overseas Registration Division, 178 Great Portland Street, London W1N 6AE.

General Dental Council (GDC)
For details about registering as a dentist, please write to:
The General Dental Council, 37 Wimpole Street, London W1M 8DQ.

The National Advice Centre for Postgraduate Dental Education (NACPDE)
For general advice on dental education after you graduate, please write to: The National Advice Centre for Postgraduate Dental Education (NACPDE), Faculty of Dental Surgery, Royal College of Surgeons of England, 35-43 Lincoln's Inn Fields, London WC2A 3PN.

The Nursing and Midwifery Council (NMC)
23 Portland Place, London, W1B 1PZ.
Telephone: 020 7333 6666
communications@nmc-uk.org
www.nmc-uk.org

TAXATION & CUSTOMS

HM Customs & Excise
For advice for travellers and businesses on imports, duties and taxes, contact:
www.hmce.gov.uk

HM Revenue and Customs
For advice on bringing personal belongings and goods into the UK, contact:
HM Revenue & Customs, Dorset House, Stamford Street, London SE1 9PY.
Telephone: (+44) (0)845 010 9000
Website: www.hmrc.gov.uk

Inland Revenue
The Inland Revenue provides advice on taxation, National Insurance Contributions, National Minimum Wage, tax credits, and Child Benefit. You can find the nearest office in the local telephone directory, or visit: www.inlandrevenue.gov.uk

GENERAL LEGAL ADVICE

Citizens' Advice Bureau
The Citizens' Advice Bureau provides free, confidential and impartial advice. They can help you solve problems including debt, housing, legal matters, and employment matters. Citizens' Advice Bureaux are in most towns. You can find them in the local telephone directory, or visit:
www.citizensadvice.org.uk

POLICE REGISTRATION & OTHER POLICE MATTERS

Registering with the police
Once you arrive in the United Kingdom, you may have to register your stay with the police. If you need to register, this requirement will be stamped in your passport. You must register within seven days of arriving in the United Kingdom. To register, you will need your passport and two passport-size photographs of yourself.

If you are staying in the Metropolitan Police Area, you should take these to: The Overseas Visitors Record Office, Brandon House, 180 Borough High Street, London SE1 1LH. The office is open between 9 am and 4:30 pm, Monday to Friday. You can get more information from the Overseas Visitors Records Office on 020 7230 1208.

If you are *not* staying in the Metropolitan Area, you should contact your local police service for the address and opening hours of other police registration offices. You will have to pay a fee for registering with the police.

Employer mistreatment
If you think your employer is exploiting or mistreating you or other workers, contact your local police station. The telephone number is in the local telephone directory.

REALLY USEFUL WEBSITES

We have listed below a number of useful websites, which we feel will be of help in searching for jobs, courses, or information about coming to the UK. There are, however, hundreds of thousands of related websites which can be accessed by a simple 'Google' search – www.google.co.uk. Go to the 'Google' site and type in 'jobs uk' and you will find that there are 70,500,000 matches! Try 'students to uk' and 51,800,000 matches are available.

DESCRIPTION	ORGANISATION	WEBSITE
Immigration Advice	Overseas Consultancy Services	www.overseasconsultancy.com
General web search	Google	www.google.co.uk
Finding a job	EURES	www.europa.eu.int
Finding a job - 700,000 jobs listed	Job Centre Plus	www.jobcentreplus.gov.uk
Finding a job - 240,000 jobs listed	Reed	www.reed.co.uk
Finding a job - 26,000 jobs listed	Britishjobs.net	www.britishjobs.net
Finding a job - 42,000 jobs listed	Fish4jobs	www.fish4.co.uk
Finding a course of study	UCAS	www.ucas.com

DESCRIPTION	ORGANISATION	WEBSITE
Newspapers	The Times	www.timesonline.co.uk
Newspapers	Guardian	jobs.guardian.co.uk
Newspapers	Independent	www.independent.co.uk
Magazines	Nursing Times	www.nursingtimes.net
Magazines	New Scientist	www.newscientist.com
Comparing UK qualifications	NARIC	www.uknrp.org.uk
English language skills	IELTS	www.ielts.org
Students - general	British Council	www.britishcouncil.org
Courses	The Secretary College	www.thesecretary.net
Personal interest	Stories about immigrants	www.movinghere.org.uk/stories
Visas & Entry Clearance	UKvisas	www.ukvisas.gov.uk/enquiries
Council for Intl Education	UKCOSA	www.ukcosa.org.uk
Nursing Information and Registration	NMC	www.nmc-uk.org
National Health Service Careers	NHS	www.nhscareers.nhs.uk
Occupation Therapy	BAOT	www.cot.org.uk
About UK	Tourist Information-UK	www.tourist-information-uk.com

APPENDICES

APPENDIX 1
SBS – LIST OF JOBS FOR WHICH WORK PERMITS CAN BE GRANTED

Work Permits UK can issue a work permit for these jobs in hospitality:

- Bar staff
- Chefs (at National Vocational Qualification level 2 and below)
- Cleaners (in staff canteens and restaurants only)
- Concierge staff
- Food service operatives (serving food)
- Housekeepers
- Kitchen assistants (preparing food, cleaning and general help)
- Room attendants
- Reception staff
- Waiting staff

Work Permits UK can issue a work permit for these jobs in food manufacturing:

- Fish filleters (preparing and cleaning fish)
- Fish packers (packing and labelling fish)
- Fish Process Operatives (operating, minding, cleaning machines that prepare fish)
- Animal gut remover
- Meat bone breaker
- Meat bone extractor
- Meat cold store operative
- Meat cutter
- Meat packer
- Meat process operatives
- Meat slaughter person
- Lairageman (pre-slaughter animal welfare attendant)
- Trimmer (trims fat from and shapes meat, after it has been boned and cut)
- Mushroom processor (tending, picking, grading and packing mushrooms)

APPENDIX 2
LIST OF SHORTAGE OCCUPATIONS FOR WHICH WORK PERMITS CAN BE GRANTED

Engineering Shortage Occupations

Railway engineers
For jobs that are listed below, the person must have a degree with at least 2 years' relevant experience from a civil, structures or electrical background: Railways Planner or Engineer; Railways Modeller; Railway Track Design or Permanent Way Engineer; Signalling Engineer, Communications Engineer; Power Supply Engineer; or Electrification Engineer.

Senior positions in the above posts would be expected to have at least 5 years' relevant experience.

Structural/bridge engineers
For jobs that are listed below, the person must have a degree with at least 2 years' relevant experience from a structures background: Structural Engineer; Infrastructure Engineer; Buildings Engineer; Bridge Engineer; or Highways Structural Engineer.

Senior posts would generally require appropriate chartered status and a minimum of 5 years' relevant experience.

Transportation and highways engineers
For jobs that are listed below, the person must have a transport related degree or a degree with at least 2 years' relevant experience from a civil background: Traffic Engineer; Transport Planner; Transport Modeller; Transport Economist – the applicant would be expected to have experience in multi-model studies & modelling software such as TRIPS, EMME2, QVIEW, SATURN, PEDROUTE or Microsimulation; Transport Signal Engineer; Highways Design Engineer; Highways Planning Engineer; Highways Maintenance Engineer.

Appendices

Healthcare Shortage Occupations

Doctors
Salaried GPs

Dentists
Salaried General Dental Practitioners; Salaried Assistant Dentists; Salaried Vocational Dental Practitioner; Consultants in Paediatric Dentistry; Consultants in Dental Specialities.

Consultant posts in the following specialist areas:
Accident and Emergency; Additional Dental Specialities; Anaesthetics; Cardiology; Cardiothoracic Surgery; Chemical Pathology; Child and Adolescent Psychiatry; Clinical Cytogenetics and Molecular Genetics; Clinical Neurophysiology; Clinical Oncology; Clinical Radiology; Dermatology; Endocrinology and Diabetes Mellitus; Endodentics; Forensic Psychiatry; Gastroenterology; General Adult Psychiatry; General Internal Medicine; General Surgery; Genito-urinary medicine; Geriatric Medicine; Haematology; Histopathology; Immunology; Infectious Diseases; Intensive Care Medicine; Medical Microbiology & Virology; Medical Oncology; Neurology; Neurosurgery; Nuclear Medicine; Obstetrics and Gynaecology; Occupational Health; Old Age Psychiatry; Opthalmology; Oral & Maxillo-facial Surgery; Orthodontics; Otolaryngology; Paediatric Cardiology; Paediatrics; Palliative Medicine; Plastic Surgery; Psychiatry of Learning Disabilities; Psychotherapy; Public Health Medicine; Rehabilitation Medicine; Renal Medicine; Respiratory Medicine; Rheumatology; Trauma and Orthopaedic Surgery; Urology.

General
Audiologist; Audiological scientist; Clinical Psychologist; Dietician; Occupational Therapist; Pharmacists; Pharmacy Technician; Physiotherapist; Speech and Language Therapist; Social Worker; Biomedical Scientist / Medical Laboratory Scientific Officer (MLSO); Qualified HPC registered Diagnostic and Therapeutic Radiographers, including ultrasonographers.

Nurses
All registered nurses and midwives.

Other occupations

Actuaries
CAA Licensed Aircraft Engineers
Teachers - all posts in England covering compulsory schooling
Veterinary Surgeons

APPENDIX 3
WHO DOES NOT REQUIRE A WORK PERMIT?

European Economic Area (EEA) nationals: Austria; Belgium; Denmark; Finland; France; Germany; Greece; Iceland; Republic of Ireland; Italy; Liechtenstein; Luxembourg; the Netherlands; Norway; Portugal; Spain; Sweden; UK).

Citizens of Switzerland.

British Overseas Territories citizens except those from Sovereign Base Areas in Cyprus. (Those included are Anguilla, Bermuda, British Antarctic Territory, British Virgin Islands, British Indian Ocean Islands, Cayman Islands, Falkland Islands and dependencies, Gibraltar, Monserrat, Pitcairn Islands, St. Helena and Dependencies, and Turks and Caicos Islands).

Commonwealth citizens who were allowed to enter or to remain in the UK on the basis that a grandparent was born here.

Spouses, unmarried partners and dependant children under 18, of people who hold work permits, or who qualify under any of the above categories, or those listed below as long as the endorsement in their passport places no restriction on their employment here.

Those who do not have any conditions attached to their stay in the UK.

Appendices

From 1 May 2004, nationals of some of the new EU Accession member states working in the UK will be subject to the Worker Registration Scheme. Where they are subject to the scheme, they need to register within one month of starting work for an employer in the UK. The following nationals will need to register: Czech; Estonian; Hungarian; Latvian; Lithuanian; Polish; Slovakian; Slovenian.

Nationals of Malta and Cyprus working in the UK are not subject to this scheme and can apply for a residence permit now.

Under the Immigration Rules, a person does not need a work permit if they qualify under one of the following categories, and they have obtained prior entry clearance at a British Diplomatic Post abroad, where necessary: those coming to the UK to set up a new business or to take over or join an existing business as a partner or director, or as a sole trader; those receiving training in techniques and work practices used in the UK, providing that the training is confined to observation, familiarisation and classroom instruction only; ministers of religion, missionaries and members of religious orders; representatives of overseas newspapers, news agencies, and broadcasting organisations; private servants in diplomatic households; representatives of overseas firms who are seeking to establish a UK branch or subsidiary; teachers and language assistants under approved exchange schemes; employees of an overseas Government coming to do a job for their Government or international organisation of which the UK is a member; seamen under contract to join a ship due to leave British waters on an international voyage; senior operational ground staff of overseas-owned airlines based at international airports; seasonal workers at agricultural camps under approved schemes; doctors, dentists, and General Practitioners in post-graduate training; entertainers and sportspeople participating in benefit matches and charity events for which there is no fee, or in international competitions; entertainers and sportspeople attending trials and auditions which do not involve a performance to a fee-paying audience (paid rehearsals do require a work permit); entertainers participating at certain festivals; working holidaymakers undertaking employment as an integral part of their holiday; Innovators; Investors; Au Pairs; Domestic Workers; Writers, Composers, and Artists.

APPENDIX 4
WORKER REGISTRATION SCHEME

How do I apply? How should I pay? You should complete application form WRS giving your name, address, date of birth, nationality, and your employment details. The charge for a first application is £50. You must fill in the payment slip on the application form. Forms and full instructions can be downloaded from the Home Office website: www.ind.homeoffice.gov.uk

You should allow up to 3 weeks from the date of application for a decision. Incomplete or complex applications may take longer.

APPENDIX 5
MORE INFORMATION FOR AU PAIRS

If you are having difficulties with your host family, you may ask your agency for help.

If you feel that you have been unfairly treated by your agency and want advice, you should contact the Employment Agency Standards Office at the Department for Trade and Industry (DTI). Their helpline number is 0645 555105, or you can write to them at 1 Victoria Street, London SW1H OET.

The following organisations may be able to help you if you are in difficulty. Those marked with a star (*) can also help you find a family who want an au pair. You can contact: your consulate (your country's representative in the UK); your local Citizens' Advice Bureau; your local Young Women's Christian Association (YWCA); and your local Young Men's Christian Association (YMCA). Their addresses and telephone numbers are in your local telephone book.

*International Catholic Society for Girls (ACISJF), 55 Nightingale Road, Rickmansworth, Hertfordshire WD3 2BU. Telephone: 01923 778449.

Appendices

Swiss Benevolent Society, 83 Marylebone High Street, London W1M 3DE. Telephone: 0207 935 1303

If you want addresses of au pair agencies, please contact: * Recruitment and Employment Confederation, 36-38 Mortimer Street, London W1N 7RB. Telephone: 020 7462 3260. (Please send a stamped addressed label or international reply coupon.)

The International Au Pair Association (IAPA), c/o FIYTO, Bredegade 25 H, DK. 1260 Copenhagen K, Denmark. Telephone: 0045 3333 9600; Fax: 0045 3393 9676. (Please say that you want addresses of agencies in the UK.)

*The British Au Pair Agencies Association (BAPAA), c/o FIYTO, Bredegade 25 H, DK. 1260 Copenhagen K, Denmark. Telephone: 0045 3333 9600; Fax: 0045 3393 9676.

APPENDIX 6
SCIENCE AND ENGINEERING GRADUATE SCHEME – ELIGIBLE SUBJECTS AT EACH LEVEL OF STUDY

The following Principal Subjects as defined in the Joint Academic Coding System (JACS) are those eligible for SEGS. Any subject with a JACS code having the same letter and first digit as a Principal Subject is considered to fall within that Principal Subject. For example the Principal Subject *H100 General Engineering* includes *H121 Fire Safety Engineering*.

Eligibility is limited to first degree programmes and to taught and research postgraduate programmes. If your programme is categorised as 'Other Undergraduate' you are not eligible regardless of the subject of your programme. The 'Other Undergraduate' category includes Higher National Certificates (HNC), Higher National Diplomas (HND), Diplomas in Higher Education (DipHE), and Foundation Degrees.

Appendices

First Degree Programmes
A100 Pre-clinical Medicine; A200 Pre-clinical Dentistry; C100 Biology; C200 Botany; C700 Molecular Biology, Biophysics and Biochemistry; D600 Food and Beverage Studies; F100 Chemistry; F200 Materials Science; F300 Physics; F600 Geology; F800 Physical and Terrestrial Geographical and Environmental Sciences; G300 Statistics; H000 Balanced Combinations in Engineering*; H100 General Engineering; H200 Civil Engineering; H700 Production and Manufacturing Engineering; H800 Chemical, Process and Energy Engineering; J100 Minerals Technology; J200 Metallurgy; J400 Polymers and Textiles; J500 Materials Technology not otherwise specified; J600 Maritime Technology; J700 Industrial Biotechnology; K200 Building; Postgraduate Taught Programmes; C200 Botany; C300 Zoology; C400 Genetics; D700 Agricultural Sciences; F000 Balanced Combinations in Physical Sciences*; F300 Physics; F500 Astronomy; G200 Operational Research; H000 Balanced Combinations in Engineering*; H100 General Engineering; H600 Electronic and Electrical Engineering; H700 Production and Manufacturing Engineering; J100 Minerals Technology; J400 Polymers and Textiles; J500 Materials Technology not otherwise specified; J600 Maritime Technology; Postgraduate Research Programmes; A100 Pre-clinical Medicine; B400 Nutrition; B500 Ophthalmics; B600 Aural and Oral Sciences; C300 Zoology; C700 Molecular Biology, Biophysics and Biochemistry; D700 Agricultural Sciences; F100 Chemistry; F200 Materials Science; H000 Balanced Combinations in Engineering*; H300 Mechanical Engineering; H400 Aerospace Engineering; H600 Electronic and Electrical Engineering; H800 Chemical, Process and Energy Engineering; J200 Metallurgy; J600 Maritime Technology

* Eligibility of programmes coded in whole or part as F000 or H000 depends on their content. See the notes for details of eligibility and how to claim it.

How do I know if my programme is eligible?
The Department for Education and Skills (DfES) has created a list of eligible Science and Engineering subjects. The list focuses on the subjects and skills that the Roberts Review identified as being in short

supply. Only those who have studied programmes in the approved subjects are eligible to apply for leave under the scheme. Approved subjects are identified by their Joint Academic Coding System (JACS) code. This system, developed jointly by the Universities and Colleges Admissions Service (UCAS, www.ucas.ac.uk) and the Higher Education Statistics Agency (HESA, www.hesa.ac.uk), is now used by institutions providing HE programmes, and by the Teaching Quality Information website (www.tqi.ac.uk).

You will need to ask your academic tutor for the JACS code that will be returned, or has been returned, to HESA as the 'Subject of qualification aim' for your programme at the point of completion. You can then check whether you are eligible by looking that code up in the list of eligible subjects.

What if my programme covers more than one subject or is broadly based?

Many degree programmes cover more than one subject, including those known as 'Joint Honours'. HESA recognises four possible patterns: single-subject; balanced two-subject combination; major/minor two-subject combination; balanced three-subject combination.

Your institution reports your programme to HESA according to the pattern that best matches it, and the match might not be exact. For example, if the second subject is a very small component, your programme is reported as single-subject, and the test for eligibility is based on that subject.

A balanced two-subject programme is eligible if one of the components is eligible, or if both are.

A major/minor programme is eligible if the major component is eligible, or if both are.

A balanced three-subject programme is eligible if two of the components are eligible, or if all three are.

Your academic tutor will be able to tell you which pattern is being used to describe your programme, and the JACS code of each component.

Some programmes are broadly-based within a subject group, and will have a 'generic JACS code' such as F000 for Physical Sciences or H000 for Engineering.

If your programme is coded in this way as a whole, then your application for the scheme must be accompanied by an official letter from your institution certifying that at least half of the material covered by the programme is eligible. The same applies if either of these two generic codes is used for one or more components of a combination programme, unless the coding of other components already establishes eligibility.

What if I have taken a BEd?

Integrated undergraduate programmes leading to Qualified Teacher Status commonly last for four years and lead to the Bachelor of Education (BEd) degree.

Such programmes are regarded as comprising one-half teacher training, which is not eligible for the scheme, and one-half subject content. If the whole of the subject content is eligible, then the programme is eligible. The subject content may lie within a single JACS Principal Subject that is eligible, or may be split across more than one.

APPENDIX 7
MORE ABOUT THE INNOVATORS APPLICATION PROCESS

You must provide: a fully completed entry clearance application form (you can get one from British missions overseas); two passport-size photographs; the correct visa fee; and a current curriculum vitae (CV).

You must also provide a business plan with supporting evidence which: explains your proposals; lets the Home Office assess if they are possible; and shows how you will bring economic benefit to the UK.

Supporting evidence which explains your proposals should be: of a high standard; from a clear source; and relevant to your application.

Here are some examples of evidence you might need: registered accounts and trading records of own business; references from your previous employer; academic certificates at or beyond your first degree; academic references; any of your research, publications, executive summary of your dissertation and so on; intellectual property rights (IPR); financial references, guarantees and forecasts; technical references; commercial references; evidence of market research you carried out; a marketing plan; evidence of the shares you will have in your proposed UK registered company; an analysis of the labour and skills you will need and your recruitment processes.

There is also a self-assessment form that you can complete and send with your application. It is designed to help the Home Office assess your application. We recommend that you use the self-assessment form when preparing your application. It can be obtained from the Innovator pages of the following website www.workingintheuk.gov.uk

APPENDIX 8
MORE ABOUT MEDICAL VISITORS

Entry Clearance Officers (ECOs) have the discretion to waive the requirement to produce evidence that arrangements have been made for treatment where they are satisfied about the means and intention to visit for private medical treatment (and leave at the end of it).

If the ECO has reason to believe that the applicant may be suffering from a communicable disease, they should refer the person for medical clearance. This applies equally to any applicant who does not give medical treatment as the reason for a visit but who suffers, or appears to suffer, from a serious disease or disability.

Can I extend my stay for a medical visit?
The normal 6 month time limit will initially apply to a visit for medical treatment. However, the Home Office can agree an extension of stay where the person continues to meet the requirements and provides evidence from a registered medical practitioner, who holds an NHS consultant post or who appears in the Specialist Register of the General Medical Council, of satisfactory arrangements/likely duration/evidence of progress of the consultation or treatment.

Where do I get information about the cost of treatment?
Where there is doubt about the costs of, or arrangements for, private treatment, you should contact the consultant or hospital in the UK direct for confirmation.

Appendices

Occasionally an ECO may decide it is appropriate to defer a decision on an application while guidance is sought from the Home Office. Examples are where an applicant has a history of mental illness or suffers from a chronic complaint and is likely to need hospital treatment, or when it is unclear whether the applicant may in fact be termed 'ordinarily resident' in the UK, and hence eligible for free NHS treatment.

All deferrals should contain as much information and documentary evidence as possible including, where relevant, a full medical report. The points on which guidance is sought should be clearly stated. The Home Office will liaise with the Department of Health as appropriate.

Can I get NHS treatment?

The general rule is that an overseas national has no claim to receive free National Health Service treatment except in the event of an accident or when requiring other emergency treatment while in the UK. Any person seeking entry for NHS treatment should normally be refused entry.

The exceptions to this general rule are contained in the Department of Health Patients Guide. There are specific reciprocal arrangements with certain countries (other than the European Economic Area, whose nationals already qualify) whereby their nationals (and in some cases residents of that country) qualify for NHS treatment of illnesses which arise while the visitors from these countries are in the UK.

Of the countries in list A below, only the nationals are eligible for treatment as described above. Both the nationals and residents of countries listed at B are eligible.

LIST A	LIST B
Bulgaria	Anguilla*
Czech Republic	Australia
Commonwealth of Independent States(except Latvia, Lithuania and Estonia)	British Virgin Islands*
	Channel Islands*
	Falkland Islands*
Gibraltar *	Hong Kong
Hungary	Iceland
Malta *	Isle of Man*
New Zealand	Montserrat*
Slovak Republic	Poland
Turkey	Romania
Yugoslavia (all territories formerly comprising)	St Helena*
	Turks and Caicos Islands*

Appendices

*Special NHS quota scheme Nationals of countries marked with an asterisk above are permitted to go to the UK on a quota basis to receive free hospital treatment. The Department of Health administers this scheme, charging the countries for each treatment after a quota has been exhausted.

If application is made for visas in such cases, the ECO will need to see evidence that proper arrangements have been made, e.g. a letter from a UK hospital or the Department of Health confirming that treatment has been agreed.

Visas issued in this category should be endorsed '*C: VISIT MEDICAL TREATMENT. LTE 6 MONTHS, CODE 3*'.

APPENDIX 9
VISA NATIONALS

Visa and Direct Airside Transit Visa (DATV) Nationals

Visa nationals are those who require a visa for every entry to the UK, though some may be able to 'Transit Without Visa'. Those who require visas for transit as well, are listed on following pages under Direct Airside transit.

Afghanistan	Gambia	Palestinian Authority
Albania	Georgia	Philippines
Algeria	Ghana	Qatar
Angola	Guinea	Romania
Armenia	Guinea Bissau	Russia
Azerbaijan	Guyana	Rwanda
Bahrain	Haiti	Sao Tome & Principe
Bangladesh	India	Saudi Arabia
Belarus	Indonesia	Senegal
Benin	Iran	Serbia & Montenegro
Bhutan	Iraq	Sierra Leone
Bosnia-Herzegovina	Ivory Coast	Somalia
Bulgaria	Jamaica	Sri Lanka
Burkina Faso	Jordan	Sudan
Burma (Myanmar)	Kazakhstan	Surinam
Burundi	Kenya	Syria

continued on next page

Appendices

Cambodia
Cameroon
Cape Verde
Central African Republic
Chad
China, People's Rep. of
Colombia
Comoros
Congo, Democratic Republic of
Congo, Republic of
Croatia
Cuba
Djibouti
Dominican Republic
Ecuador
Egypt
Equatorial Guinea
Eritrea
Ethiopia
Fiji
Gabon
Korea (Dem. People's Rep)
Kuwait
Kyrgyzstan
Laos
Lebanon
Liberia
Libya
Macedonia
Madagascar
Mali
Mauritania
Moldova
Mongolia
Morocco
Mozambique
Nepal
Niger
Nigeria
Oman
Pakistan
Peru
Taiwan
Tajikistan
Tanzania
Thailand
Togo
Tunisia
Turkey
'Turkish Republic of Northern Cyprus'
Turkmenistan
Uganda
Ukraine
United Arab Emirates
Uzbekistan
Vatican City (service & emergency passports only)
Vietnam
Yemen
Zambia
Zimbabwe

Since 13 November 2003 nationals of ten 'phase one' countries require entry clearance for all stays of more than six months. The 'phase one' countries are: Australia, Canada, Hong Kong SAR, Japan, Malaysia, New Zealand, Singapore, South Africa, South Korea, and USA.

Appendices

Direct Airside Transit Visa (DATV) Nationals

In addition to needing a visa to enter the UK, nationals of the following countries also require a visa to transit through the UK, known as Direct Airside Transit (DATV).

Afghanistan
Albania
Algeria
Angola
Bangladesh
Belarus
Burma
Burundi
Cameroon
China, Peoples Republic of
Colombia
Congo
Congo, Democratic Republic of
Ecuador
Eritrea
Ethiopia
Gambia
Ghana
Guinea
Guinea-Bissau
India
Iran
Iraq
Ivory Coast
Kenya
Lebanon
Liberia
Macedonia
Moldova
Mongolia
Nepal
Nigeria
Palestinian Authority
Pakistan
Rwanda
Senegal
Serbia and Montenegro
    (including documents issued by
    the United Nations Mission in Kosovo)
Sierra Leone
Sudan
Somalia
Sri Lanka
Tanzania
Turkey
'Turkish Republic of Northern Cyprus'
Uganda
Vietnam
Zimbabwe

Passengers exempt from the DATV requirement.

Holders of certain documents are, regardless of nationality, exempt from the requirement to hold a Direct Airside Transit Visa when transiting the UK.

A transit passenger is not required to hold a transit visa if he holds, or a person with whom he arrives in the UK holds on his behalf: a valid visa for entry to Australia, Canada, New Zealand, or the United States of America, and a valid airline ticket for travel via the UK as part of a journey from another country or territory to the country in respect of which the visa is held; a valid visa for entry to Australia, Canada, New Zealand, or the United States of America, and a valid airline ticket for travel via the UK as part of a journey from the country in respect of which the visa is held to another country or territory; a valid airline ticket for travel via the UK as part of a journey from Australia, Canada, New Zealand, or the United States of America, to another country or territory, provided that the transit passenger does not seek to transit the UK on a date more than six months from the date on which he last entered Australia, Canada, New Zealand, or the United States of America with a valid visa for entry to that country; a valid USA I-551 Permanent Resident Card issued on or after 21st April 1998; a valid Canadian Permanent Resident Card issued on or after 28th June 2002; a valid common format Category D visa for entry to an EEA State; a valid common format residence permit issued by an EEA State pursuant to Council Regulation (EC) No. 1030/2002; a diplomatic or service passport issued by the People's Republic of China; or a diplomatic or official passport issued by India; or, a diplomatic or official passport issued by Vietnam.

Notes:
A valid U.S. immigrant visa packet (form 155A/155B) is a 'valid visa for DATV exemption purposes. An expired I-551 Permanent Resident Card issued on or after 21 April 1998 when accompanied by an I-797 letter issued by the Bureau of Citizenship authorising its extension, exempts the holder from the DATV requirement. Holding either an I-512 Parole letter or an I-797C (Notice of Action) instead of a valid U.S. visa; or a Transportation Letter instead of a valid U.S. Permanent Residence Card issued on or after 21 April 1998 does NOT qualify for exemption from the DAT visa requirement. Holding a valid travel document with a U.S. ADIT stamp worded – 'Processed for I-551. TEMPORARY EVIDENCE OF LAWFUL ADMISSION FOR PERMANENT RESIDENCE VALID UNTIL.... EMPLOYMENT AUTHORIZED' does NOT qualify for exemption from the DAT visa requirement. Whether holders of non-national (including refugee travel documents) require a DATV depends on their nationality and whether they qualify for one of the exemptions listed above. So, for instance,

the holder of a non-national travel document (e.g. a refugee travel document) who is a national or a citizen of one of the countries listed on the DATV list (e.g. Afghanistan) will require a direct airside transit visa if they are travelling to the UK to transit on to a third country. Transiting to the Republic of Ireland Passengers must pass through immigration control in order to take a flight to Ireland. Visa nationals (and passengers qualifying for DATV exemption above) may Transit without Visa providing they fulfil the TWOV conditions and are properly documented for entry into Ireland. DATV nationals transiting to Ireland must obtain a visit visa – not a Visitor in Transit visa which is only for transit to a destination outside the Common Travel Area (Rules HC395 paragraph 47 refers). All visa nationals wishing to transit the UK but spend longer doing so than the 24 hours permitted under the TWOV concession must obtain a visitor in transit visa for stays up to 48 hours or a visit visa.

APPENDIX 10
INFORMATION ON THE RIGHT OF ABODE

If you have the right of abode in the UK, this means that you are entirely free from UK immigration control. You do not need to obtain the permission of an immigration officer to enter the UK, and you may live and work here without restriction.

However, you must prove your claim by production of either: a) a passport describing you as a British citizen or as a citizen of the UK and Colonies having the right of abode in the UK; or b) a certificate of entitlement to the right of abode in the UK issued by or on behalf of the Government of the UK.

Information about obtaining a UK passport is available from the UK Passport Service on its website at www.passport.gov.uk or by telephoning 0870 521 0410.

Who has the right of abode?
Under Section 2 of the Immigration Act 1971 (which was amended by Section 39 of the British Nationality Act 1981), all British citizens and certain Commonwealth citizens have the right of abode in the UK.

Appendices

People who became British citizens on 1 January 1983
You will have become a British citizen on 1 January 1983 (when the British Nationality Act 1981 came into force), and will therefore have the right of abode in the UK if, immediately before that date: a) you were a citizen of the UK and Colonies and had your citizenship by being born, adopted, naturalised or registered (see Note 4) in the UK; or b) (i) you were a citizen of the UK and Colonies with a parent (see Note 2) who, at the time of your birth, was a citizen of the UK and Colonies by being born, adopted, naturalised or registered (see Note 4) in the UK; or (ii) you were a citizen of the UK and Colonies whose parent (see Note 2) qualified for the right of abode under b (i) above; or c) you were a citizen of the UK and Colonies who, at any time before 31 December 1982, had been ordinarily resident in the UK (see Note 1) for a continuous period of 5 years or more and, during that period, you were not in breach of the immigration laws and, at the end of that period, you did not have any time limit attached to your stay; or d) you were a citizen of the UK and Colonies and were then, or had previously been, the wife of a man with the right of abode in the UK.

People who became British citizens after 1 January 1983
A person born in the UK (see Note 1) after 1 January 1983 is a British citizen if his father or mother (see Note 2) was, at that time: a) a British citizen; or b) settled (see Note 5) in the UK.

A person born outside the UK (see Note 1) after 1 January 1983 is a British citizen if, at the time of his birth, his father (see Note 2) or mother was: a) a British citizen otherwise than by descent; or b) a British citizen by descent and was in (i) Crown service, or (ii) Community institution service, or (iii) service specially designated by the Secretary of State as being closely associated with the activities of the UK government.

A person who has successfully applied for registration or naturalisation as a British citizen will have become such a citizen on the date of registration or, as the case may be, the date of issue of the certificate of naturalisation.

A person adopted in the UK after 1 January 1983 is a British citizen if, on the date of the adoption, at least one of the adopters was a British citizen.

Appendices

If you are not a British citizen, you could still have the right of abode if you are a Commonwealth citizen and, on 31 December 1982: a) you were a Commonwealth citizen with a parent (see Note 2) who, at the time of your birth or legal adoption (see Note 3), was a citizen of the UK and Colonies and had his/her citizenship by being born in the UK (see Note 1); or b) you were a Commonwealth citizen and are, or were, the wife of a man with the right of abode.

Note: If you were not a Commonwealth citizen on 31 December 1982 or you ceased to be a Commonwealth citizen (even temporarily) at any time after that date, you will not have the right of abode. For example, nationals of South Africa and Pakistan do not qualify because these countries left the Commonwealth before 1983 and rejoined afterwards.

Certificates of Entitlement

A certificate of entitlement to right of abode in the UK is a gummed sticker that is fixed in a valid passport. It constitutes proof of your right of abode for UK immigration control purposes.

The Home Office issues certificates of entitlement to eligible applicants in the UK. If you are abroad, you should apply to the nearest British Diplomatic Post. A list of such Posts is available on the Foreign and Commonwealth Office website at www.fco.gov.uk .

In both cases, a fee is payable for processing applications (see below).

How do I apply for a certificate of entitlement to the right of abode in the UK?

Applications made in the UK for a certificate of entitlement to the right of abode are dealt with by the Integrated Casework Directorate, which is based in Liverpool. Your claim will be examined and a certificate of entitlement to the right of abode in the UK will be issued if you qualify for one, provided you have produced satisfactory original documentary evidence and have paid the application fee. Please note that it can take up to three months or more to process an application and you should allow for this when applying.

Information you give will be treated in confidence but may be shared with other government departments, agencies, and local authorities, so they can carry out their own work.

Appendices

There is a right of appeal against refusal to issue a certificate of entitlement. If your application is not successful, the Home Office will write to you about this when they inform you of the decision.

Fees

A fee of £20 is required for EACH passport requiring a certificate of entitlement to the right of abode in the UK. If more than one person travels on the same passport, only one fee is payable.

Transfers of certificate of entitlement to the right of abode in the UK

If you have a certificate of patriality or a certificate of entitlement to the right of abode in the UK in an old passport, and you want it transferred to a new passport, you should send both your old and new passports to the Integrated Casework Directorate with a letter asking for the transfer to be done, and 2 passport-size photographs.

You should: briefly explain how you qualify for the right of abode, and give a telephone number so we can contact you in case we have a query. You do not have to pay a fee to have a certificate of entitlement or patriality transferred into your new passport.

NOTES

1. UK means: England, Wales, Scotland, Northern Ireland, the Channel Islands, and the Isle of Man; and the Republic of Ireland at a time when it formed part of the UK (that is to say, before 31 March 1922); and (in relation to birth) a ship or aircraft registered in the UK or an unregistered ship or aircraft of the Government of the UK.

2. Parent includes: the mother, but not the father, of an illegitimate child (a child born out of wedlock may be legitimated by the subsequent marriage of his or her parents); the adoptive parents of a child who has been legally adopted (see Note 3).

3. Legal adoption means adoption by order of a court in the UK and Islands (i.e. the Channel Islands or the Isle of Man) or in any country specified by the Secretary of State under section 72(2) of the Adoption Act 1976. These countries and territories are:

Appendices

Anguilla	Fiji	Malawi	St Christopher &
Australia	Finland	Malaysia	Nevis St Vincent
Austria	France	Malta	Surinam
Bahamas	Germany	Mauritius	Swaziland
Barbados	Ghana	Montserrat	Sweden
Belgium	Gibraltar	Namibia	Switzerland
Belize	Greece	Netherlands	Tanzania
Bermuda	Guyana	New Zealand	Tonga
Botswana	Hong Kong	Nigeria	Trinidad & Tobago
British Virgin Islands	Iceland	Norway	Turkey
Canada	Ireland (Rep)	Pitcairn	Uganda
Cayman Islands	Israel	Portugal	United States of
China	Italy	Seychelles	America
Cyprus (Rep)	Jamaica	Singapore	Yugoslavia
Denmark	Kenya	South Africa	Zambia
Dominica	Lesotho	Spain	Zimbabwe
	Luxembourg	Sri Lanka	

A child of any nationality who was adopted in the UK on or after 1 January 1950, or in the Channel Islands or the Isle of Man on or after 1 April 1959, automatically became a citizen of the UK and Colonies on his adoption if the adoptive father (or adoptive mother, if she was the sole adopter) was a citizen of the UK and Colonies at the time of the adoption.
4. Registration in the UK includes registration at the High Commission of an independent Commonwealth country.

It does not include: registration under section 6(2) of the British Nationality Act 1948 (registration on the grounds of marriage to a citizen of the UK and Colonies) if the marriage took place after 28.10.71; or registration under section 7 of the British Nationality Act 1948 (registration of minors) at a High Commission after 28.10.71; or registration under section 12 (6) of the British Nationality Act 1948 at a High Commission
5. Settled in the UK means being ordinarily resident in the UK without being subject to any time limit under the immigration laws. A person is not settled if he or she: is in the UK in breach of the immigration laws; or is exempt from immigration control because he or she is a member of a diplomatic or consular mission, visiting forces, or an international organisation; or has only a conditional right of residence under European Community law – for example as a worker or student.

APPENDIX 11
SAMPLE HSMP CALCULATOR
POINTS HSMP CANDIDATES

Candidate's Name: _____

POINTS

If you are under 28 years of age you will gain
5 additional points.

....

Qualification
- o PhD – 30 points
- o Masters Degree (e.g. MBA) – 25 points
- o Graduate degree (e.g. BA or BSc) – 15 points
- o None of the above – 0 points

......

Work Experience
- o At least 5 years full time graduate level work experience (or 3 years if you have a Phd – 25 points
- o At least 5 years full time graduate level work experience including at least 2 years' in a senior or specialist role – 35 points
- o At least 10 years full time graduate level work experience including at least 5 years' in a senior or specialist role – 50 points

......

Income over the last twelve months in UK Currency

o ....

Country of Residence over the last twelve months (where you have derived the 12 months income)

o ....

....

Spouse / unmarried partner educated to degree level
or previously employed in a graduate level job
and lived together for 2 years or more – 10 points

......

TOTAL POINTS ___